2022
DEC — REC'D

RIP CHADWICK BOSEMAN

D1521061

Boseman's career was revolutionary and he leaves behind a game-changing legacy. Chadwick Boseman began his career playing African American icons and pioneers; he ends it as one himself. His achievements, as an actor and as a cultural force, will surely prove to be as heroic as those of the characters he portrayed. At the very least, he leaves the film-making landscape looking very different to how it was when he entered it.

JOURNEY TO WAKANDA
BLACK PANTHER & BEYOND....
THE LIFE and LEGACY of
CHADWICK BOSEMAN

JOURNEY TO WAKANDA
BLACK PANTHER & BEYOND....
THE LIFE and LEGACY of
CHADWICK BOSEMAN

TONY ROSE AND YVONNE ROSE

COLOSSUS BOOKS
A Division of Amber Communications Group, Inc.
New York   Phoenix   Los Angeles

JOURNEY TO WAKANDA, BLACK PANTHER & BEYOND....
THE LIFE and LEGACY of CHADWICK BOSEMAN

Published by: Colossus Books

Phoenix, Arizona

www.amberbookspublishing.com

Tony Rose, Publisher / Editorial Director
Yvonne Rose, Editor

© Copyright 2023 by Amber Communications Group, Inc.

ISBN #: 978-1-0880-0015-1

Library of Congress Control Number: 2022920446

Printed in the United States of America

DEDICATION

To the Fans of
Chadwick Boseman
and
Black Panther

CONTENTS

PREFACE

IT WAS HIS TIME!

*B*efore Chadwick Boseman gained worldwide notoriety and recognition for playing T'Challa, the King of the fictional African nation Wakanda, he was known around Hollywood for being the go-to man for a biopic. Boseman was best known for his portrayal of Jackie Robinson in 42, James Brown in Get on Up, and Thurgood Marshall in Marshall.

The Howard University graduate became a growing household name, by successfully breaking into the Marvel Cinematic Universe to be the first black actor to play a lead role in a superhero movie, while being a source of inspiration for African American children and children worldwide.

After years of acting in one biopic after another, Chadwick Boseman's role as Black Panther in the "Avengers" films and the 2018 eponymous blockbuster, **Black Panther**, the ninth highest-grossing movie of all time, established him as the rare breed of actor with star power.

In the 2019 Golden Globe Awards, "Black Panther" ended up taking home the award for Outstanding Performance by a Cast in a Motion Picture as well as Outstanding Action Performance by a Stunt Ensemble in a Motion Picture.

In his acceptance speech, Boseman touched on the significance of the film in an industry historically dominated by white actors and directors. "When I think of going to work every day and the passion and the intelligence, the resolve, the discipline, that everyone showed, I also think of two questions that we all have received during the course of multiple publicity runs."

The questions were whether they thought the film would receive the kind of reception it did and whether *Black Panther* had changed the way the industry works.

Boseman responded: "My answer to that is to be young, gifted, and black... we all know what it's like to be told that there is not a place for you to be featured. Yet, you are young, gifted, and black. We know what it's like to be told that there's not a screen for you to be featured on, a stage for you to be featured on. We know what it's like to be the tail and not the head. We know what it's like to be beneath and not above."

"That is what we went to work with every day, because we knew, not that we would be around during awards season or that it would make a billion dollars, but we knew that we had something special that we wanted to give the world," he continued. "That we could be full human beings in the roles that we were playing, that we could create a world that exemplified a world that we wanted to see. And to come to work every day and to solve problems with this group of people, this director, that is something that I wish all actors would get the opportunity to experience. If you get to experience that, you will be a fulfilled artist."

CHAPTER 1

THE BEGINNING...

Chadwick Aaron Boseman, a Sagittarian was born November 29, 1977 in The Upstate area of Anderson, South Carolina. "Chad" got his middle name from his paternal grandfather Aaron

Boseman. The Boseman family was close-knit and very extensive. When Chadwick's grandmother died, she left 115 grandkids and great grandkids; and that was just one side of the family. Chadwick is from South Carolina, but one day he did a DNA test and found out his ancestors were Krio people, Limba people and Yoruba people from West Africa, including parts of Sierra Leone, Guinea-Bissau, and Nigeria.

However, his parents, Carolyn and Leroy Boseman are both African American (born in the U.S.A.). Chadwick's mother was a nurse. Chadwick saw his father work a lot of third shifts, a lot of night shifts; he worked at a textile factory, and also had a side business as an upholsterer. Chadwick once stated that "Whenever I work a particularly hard week, I think of him."

Chadwick was the youngest of three boys, who were raised as Christians. He was baptized, and was part of a church choir and youth group at the Welfare Baptist Church. Chadwick's former pastor said that he always kept his faith. He studied Hebrew and had a good knowledge of both the Old Testament and New Testament. Boseman had prayed to be the Black Panther before he was cast as the character in the Marvel Cinematic Universe.

His closest role models were his two brothers. Derrick, the eldest, is now a pastor in Murfreesboro Tennessee; and Kevin in the middle, is an accomplished dancer and choreographer based in New York City who has performed with the Martha Graham and Alvin Ailey troupes. His credits also include a stint on Broadway in *The Lion King.*

Kevin, Derrick & Chadwick

Both brothers, each five years apart from the next, were allies and rivals. Chadwick always wanted to beat Derrick in sports. And he wanted to dress better than Kevin, who ultimately foreshadowed Chadwick's life in the arts. He had always insisted that he had something and was going to do it anyway, right or wrong, and as Chadwick said, "He was right."

Kevin had the resolve, and despite the odds, he persisted in his chosen career and ultimately, excelled. In Anderson in the 1980s there was little context for a boy who dreamed of becoming a dancer, let alone a black one, and it wasn't something that his family understood. However, in time, they came around, helping Kevin get into the Governor's School for the Arts and Humanities in nearby Greenville.

Some days, Chadwick's mother would take him with her to pick up his brother Kevin from school theater or dance rehearsals. Chadwick would watch the action onstage, mesmerized by verbal directions, which he strained to understand, and by the lights; and he became awed by the excitement of show business.

Chadwick attended T. L. Hanna High School, located outside the Anderson city limits at 2600 Highway 81 North. Anderson is a city in, and the county seat of, Anderson County, South Carolina, United States. At the census of 2000, there were 25,514 people, 10,641 households, and 6,299 families residing in the city. The population density was 1,843.7 people per square mile. There were 12,068 housing units at an average density of 872.1 per square mile. The primary racial makeup of the city was 63.12% White and 34.01% African American.

Anderson became one of the first cities in the Southeastern United States to have electricity, which was established by William C. Whitner in 1895 at a hydroelectric plant on the Rocky River, giving the city the name "The Electric City." It also became the first city in the world to supply a cotton gin by electricity. Anderson is known as "The Friendliest City in South Carolina" and because of Its spirit and quality of life Anderson County earned national recognition being named an "All-America City" in 2000.

T.L. Hanna was Anderson School District 5's all-white high school (Westside was the African-American school). T.L. Hanna High gained national notoriety when James "Radio" Kennedy's story was made into a movie, in which Radio was portrayed by Cuba Gooding Jr. Radio was a young man with an intellectual disability who befriended T. L. Hanna Coach Harold Jones in 1964. Although Radio was not a student at Hanna, he and the coach became great friends, and Radio became a legend in Anderson.

In 1971, the district was integrated, nearly 20 years after the Supreme Court's 1954 ruling in Brown v. Board of Education. In 1989, T. L. Hanna High School was named "Palmetto's Finest" by the South Carolina Department of Education. In 1992, the school moved to its current location on Highway 81.

Chadwick was always ambitious, creative and determined; as a child, he wanted to become an architect. As a youth as well as an adult, he practiced martial arts. But, most memorably, while in high school, Chadwick was a serious basketball player. The Amateur Athletic Union, or AAU, is the United States' pre-eminent youth basketball organization. Teams from different towns, cities, and neighborhoods form independently (meaning not representing schools) and play each other in games and tournaments. In the summer of 1993, the 16-and-under AAU basketball squad from Anderson, S.C., made it all the way to a national competition in Orlando, Fla. It didn't produce any future NBA players, but it did feature two stars: two-time NFL Pro Bowler Shaun Ellis, and King T'Challa himself, Chadwick Boseman, or just "Chad" as he was known at the time.

A major highlight of Chad's youth basketball years was going head-to-head against another South Carolina player named Kevin Garnett, future NBA superstar, basketball Hall of Famer, and Uncut Gems star Kevin Garnett. Years later, Chadwick said on *Jimmy Kimmel Live*, "I played against Garnett in AAU. He probably would not remember it. I didn't match up with him, but I scored on him. I did an up and under on him."

However, Chadwick made a final turn toward storytelling after a friend and teammate was tragically shot and killed. He processed his thoughts and emotions; and in 1991, while in his junior year, his passion for acting and directing was realized. After the tragedy, he wrote and staged his first play, *Crossroads,* at their school. Chadwick graduated from T.L. Hanna High school in 1995.

Having been inspired by his brother Kevin's career in entertainment, Chadwick stated, "There's no way in the world I would have thought, 'O.K. let me write this play', if it wasn't for him. Ultimately, I'm here because of what Kevin did." When it was time to consider colleges, Chadwick chose an arts program at Howard University, with a dream of becoming a director.

In 2000, T.L. Hanna High was named a National Blue Ribbon School by the U.S. Department of Education. In 2014, *U.S. News & World Report* named T.L. Hanna as the fifth best high school in South Carolina and ranked it in the top 3% of high schools in the United States.

All in all, the small town school had some pretty notable alumni, including: Chadwick Boseman, actor, writer, and director, *Marshall, 42, Get On Up, Draft Day, Captain America: Civil War,* Black Panther and *Ma Rainey's Black Bottom*; James Michael Tyler, actor who played Gunther on the sitcom "Friends"; Martavis Bryant, wide receiver for Oakland Raiders of NFL; Jim Rice, Baseball Hall of Fame player for Boston Red Sox, who attended his final year of high school there in 1971; and Stephen D. Thorne, NASA astronaut.

CHAPTER 2

EDUCATION CAME FIRST

His time at Howard University helped shape both the man and the artist
that he became, committed to truth, integrity, and a determination to
transform the world through the power of storytelling.
- The Boseman Family

Chadwick Boseman's success did not come overnight. He put many years into studying and honing his craft. After high school, he attended college at Howard University in Washington, DC, a historically black higher institution of learning.

Founded in 1867, Howard University is a private, research university that is comprised of 13 schools and colleges. Howard University's historic main campus sits on a hilltop in Northwest Washington, blocks from the storied U Street and Howard Theatre. They are two miles from the U.S. Capitol where many students intern, and scores of alumni shape national and foreign policy.

Since 1867, Howard University has awarded more than 120,000 degrees in the professions, arts, sciences and humanities. Howard ranks among the highest producers of the nation's Black professionals in medicine, dentistry, pharmacy, engineering, nursing, architecture, religion, law, music, social work and education.

Howard University operates with a commitment to Excellence in Truth and Service and since its founding, has produced one Schwarzman Scholar, three Marshall Scholars, four Rhodes Scholars, 12 Truman Scholars, 25 Pickering Fellows and more than 165 Fulbright recipients. Howard also produces more on-campus African-American Ph.D. recipients than any other university in the United States.

Howard University is dedicated to educating students from diverse backgrounds. The university's undergraduate, graduate, professional, and joint degree programs span more than 120 areas of study within 13 schools and colleges, The National Science Foundation has ranked Howard as the top producer of African-American undergraduates who later earn science and engineering doctoral degrees. The University also boasts nationally ranked programs in social work, business and communications.

Regarded as one of the most prestigious institutions of higher learning, Howard University traditionally has had the largest gathering of Black scholars in the world. The university's current enrollment approximates 11,000 students from virtually every state, the District of Columbia, and more than 70 countries.

The Department of Theatre Arts (formerly the Department of Drama) developed and expanded from course offerings in Speech, and by 1870 there had been developed an annual departmental oratorical contest. Initially, public speaking was an extracurricular activity without credit. On December 5, 1874, however, the University began granting academic credit for this work.

In 1899, public speaking was extended beyond elocution to include review of elementary sounds, position of the body, breathing, production of tone inflection, modulation and emphasis. This work was implemented under the supervision of Coralie Franklin Cook, a graduate of the National School of Oratory, Philadelphia. Such was the beginning of the intensive study of public speaking as an art at the University, although it was not made compulsory until February 8, 1911.

Ernest Everett Just came to the University in 1909 as an instructor of English and, together with a number of students, organized the first drama group, the College Dramatic Club. For several years, this club gave performances annually at the Howard Theatre, a local legitimate theatre in Washington, D.C. The financial success of the College Dramatic Club was evidenced by its donation of a clock to the Andrew Carnegie Library, formerly the School of Religion.

During the period from 1919 to 1925, drama at the University reached a peak both financially and technically. In 1919, T. Montgomery Gregory was appointed head of the Department of Speech. Under his direction, courses in Dramatic Art were offered for academic credit for the first time and the College Dramatic Club became known as the Howard Players. The practical work of acting, character portrayal, technical work for the stage, the making of costumes and production management became the course offerings in Dramatic Art. The Department had its own business office, costume rooms and scenic workshop.

The Players specialized in the production of plays of Negro life written by students and others. Probably one of the most notable achievements of the Howard Players was the presentation of Emperor Jones with Charles Gilpin recreating his original role.

During the period of 1919 to 1949 the Howard Players presented countless performances written by a diverse and international spectrum of playwrights. In 1949, under the leadership of Anne Cook, the Howard Players became the first college drama group to serve as ambassadors of goodwill, as they toured two plays throughout Norway, Sweden, Denmark and Germany for a three-month period.

During newly-appointed Owen Dodson's tenure as chairman, the Departments of Drama, Art and Music merged to form the College of Fine Arts and in 1960 the three moved into the newly erected Lulu Vere Childers Hall with its adjacent Ira Aldridge Theater.

In the summer of 1973, T.G. Cooper, Chairman of the Department of Drama at that time, received a faculty research grant for a pilot program in Children's Theatre, which enabled the Department to engage the services of Professor Kelsey E. Collie. Under the expertise of Professors Cooper and Collie, the Howard University Children's Theatre received the Winifred Ward Prize as the most outstanding new Children's Theatre in the United States in 1974. The touring program performed in the 1977 Dundalk International Maytime Festival, Republic of Ireland, where they received the

President's Award, the festival's highest honor and in the 1979 Dundalk International Maytime Festival, they received the Premiere Award as best production and also won the Best Costume Award. In 1992, upon the recommendation of the faculty and the Dean of the College of Fine Arts, the Board of Trustees approved the change in name from the Department of Drama to the Department of Theatre Arts.

Howard University's dedication to cultivating talented artists has had a deep and profound impact on historical and contemporary culture.

Other famous alumni of Howard University include: Vice President Kamala Harris; Taraji P. Henson (actress), Toni Morrison (author), Zorah Neale Hurston (author), Sean Combs (entertainment executive), Anthony Anderson (actor), Debbie Allen (dance choreographer/actress), Senator Ed Brooke, Representative Elijah Cummings, Vernon Jordan (activist), Jessye Norman (opera singer), Mayor David Dinkins, Donny Hathaway (musician), Roberta Flack (musician), Stokely Carmichael/ Kwame Ture (activist), Lynn Whitfield (actress), Ossie Davis (actor), Paul Laurence Dunbar (author), Thurgood Marshall (Supreme Court Justice), Amiri Baku (author) and Phylicia Rashad (actress/educator).

After much soul-searching and many hours of research Chadwick embarked upon his chosen career path. He enrolled at Howard University in Washington, D.C. in 1998 and graduated in 2000 with a Bachelor of Fine Arts in directing. Chadwick wanted to write and direct, thus he initially began studying acting to learn how to relate to actors. But apparently all that changed when he took an acting class presented by the Tony Award-winning actress and director Phylicia Rashad. The actress best known for portraying Clair

Huxtable on The Cosby Show soon became Chadwick Boseman's mentor.

Phylicia Rashad had graduated magna cum laude in 1970 with a Bachelor of Fine Arts degree. Eighteen years later, as one of Chadwwick's teachers at Howard University, she would become his mentor. Phylicia Rashad is one of many Howard University alumni who have transformed the arts and entertainment industry through legendary careers on screen and behind the scenes, in front of the microphone and from within the boardroom. On July 21, 2021 after a comprehensive national search, Howard University appointed Phylicia Rashad as dean of the recently reestablished College of Fine Arts.

A native of Houston, Texas, Phylicia Rashad was well-respected in the academic world. She became the first recipient of the Denzel Washington Chair in Theatre at Fordham University and received an Honorary Doctorate from Spelman College the year First Lady Michelle Obama delivered the 2011 commencement address. Ms. Rashad conducted Master Classes at the prestigious Ten Chimneys Foundation for the 2015 Lunt Fontanne Fellows. She also holds Honorary Doctorates from Fordham University, Carnegie Mellon University, Howard University, Providence College, Morris Brown College, Clark Atlanta University, Barber Scotia College, St. Augustine College, and Brown University.

Inducted into the Theater Hall of Fame in 2016, Ms. Rashad received the 2016 Lucille Lortel Award for Outstanding Leading Actress in a Play for her performance as "Shelah" in Tarell Alvin McCraney's *Head of Passes* at the Public Theater.

Ms. Rashad also received both the Drama Desk and the Tony Award for Best Actress in a Play for her riveting performance as "Lena Younger" in the Broadway revival of Lorraine Hansberry's *A Raisin in The Sun.* She appeared in Ryan Coogler's *Creed,* Tyler Perry's *Good Deeds,* and starred in Perry's highly acclaimed film version of Ntozake Shange's *For Colored Girls Who Have Considered Suicide When The Rainbow Is Enuf.*

In 2015, Ms. Rashad received the BET Honors Theatrical Arts Award, Chicago Shakespeare Theatre's Spirit of Shakespeare Award, and the Inaugural Legacy Award of the Ruben Santiago Hudson Fine Arts Learning Center. Among the other awards that decorate her walls and shelves are the 2014 Mosaic Woman Legend Award of *Diversity Woman* Magazine, the Texas Medal of Arts, the National Council of Negro Women's Dorothy L. Height Dreammaker Award, AFTRA's AMEE Award for Excellence in Entertainment, the Board of Directors of New York Women In Film and Television's Muse Award for Outstanding Vision and Achievement, Dallas Women In Film Topaz Award, Peoples' Choice Awards, several NAACP Image Awards, and the Pan African Film Festival's Lifetime Achievement Award.

Whether she is bringing laughter to millions of television viewers around the world, moving theatre-goers to tears, thrilling movie fans, offering new insights to students by teaching Master Classes at renowned learning institutions that include Howard University, Julliard, and Carnegie Mellon, serving on Boards of prestigious organizations, or breaking new ground as a director, Phylicia Rashad is one of the entertainment world's most extraordinary performing artists.

Upon looking back on the relationship between the student and the teacher it's easy to acknowledge that Phylicia Rashad, is one of the primary reasons Chadwick became a huge star. He intended to pursue a career as a director and graduated from Howard University with a bachelor's degree in directing. However, he then took a course led by esteemed actress Phylicia Rashad, who influenced his decision to change career goals and become an actor. If he hadn't taken her class, he might not have become an actor or the iconic Black Panther we know him as.

While he was studying with Phylicia Rashad, Chadwick and some of his classmates were accepted for an elite theater program, the Oxford Mid-Summer Program of the British American Drama Academy in London. However, they didn't have the necessary funding; but Phylicia pushed for the students and helped fund it as well. "She pushed for us," Boseman told Rolling Stone, adding, "She essentially got some celebrity friends to pay for us to go." Most notably was prominent actor Denzel Washington.

After Chadwick finished up the program, he received a beneficiary letter and figured out who had paid for him to attend. He learned that Phylicia's friend, Denzell Washington, had been a major contributor to his funding. He wrote Washington a thank you letter, but never gave it to him, and never told anyone else about it.

More than 20 years later, at the *Black Panther* film premiere, the two met and Chadwick finally was able to express his gratitude to Denzel in person. Shortly after the film's premiere, when Chadwick was on The Tonight Show, he told Jimmy Fallon that he has "basically been holding this secret [his] whole career," because Chadwick didn't want Washington to feel like he owed him anything else. He said that he wanted to meet him in person before saying anything, but after 20 years he felt like it would be okay to reveal it to the world.

Chadwick on the Tonight Show with Jimmy Fallon

Chadwick also revealed to Jimmy Fallon on The "Tonight Show" that he finally got to meet Denzell at the New York premiere of Black Panther, which was an "amazing" experience. Chadwick told Jimmy Fallon that he thanked Denzell for paying for his Oxford experience over two decades ago. In response, Denzell replied in jest, "Oh, so that's why I'm here. You owe me money! I came to collect!"

When Chadwick attended the Oxford Mid-Summer program in 1998, he developed an appreciation for the playwriting of William Shakespeare, and for studying the works of various dramatists including Samuel Beckett and Harold Pinter. Chadwick also traveled to Africa for the first time while at college, working in Ghana with his professor Mike Malone "to preserve and celebrate rituals with performances on a proscenium stage." According to Chadwick, working in Ghana was "one of the most significant learning experiences of his life". After he returned to the U.S., he took additional course work in film studies and also graduated from New York City's Digital Film Academy.

Chadwick was goal-oriented and responsible; always planning ahead. While at college he worked in a black bookstore near the university, He drew on his experience there for *Hieroglyphic Graffiti, one of many plays which he* wrote and directed.

After studying directing at Howard University, Boseman began his career in theatre, winning a Drama League Directing Fellowship and an acting AUDELCO, along with receiving a Jeff Award nomination for his play *Deep Azure*.

During his two-decade career, Boseman also received two Screen Actors Guild Awards, a Golden Globe Award, and a Critics' Choice Movie Award, among other accolades. He was also posthumously nominated for an Academy Award and a Primetime Emmy Award.

In 2018, Chadwick Boseman rocketed to international fame as King T'Challa in the Marvel movie "Black Panther".

That same year, eighteen years after he graduated from Howard University, on May 12th Chadwick Boseman gave the commencement address at Howard University, at which time he was awarded the degree of Doctor of Humane Letters (DHL), which is an honorary degree awarded to those who have distinguished themselves through humanitarian and philanthropic contributions to society.

When Chadwick Boseman returned to the Howard campus to serve as the commencement speaker, he called Howard a "magical place". During Chadwick's visit, Howard University President Wayne A. I. Frederick announced plans to return its performing and visual arts school to its independent status as the Department of Theatre Arts.

That announcement was music to Chadwick's ears. For years, he had led the movement to keep the College of Fine Arts from being integrated into the College of Arts & Sciences. Finally, those efforts would be fulfilled…and there was more to come…but sadly, Chadwick would not be there to bear witness.

In the days following Chadwick's death, Howard students circulated a petition to have the fine arts college renamed for him. Unbeknownst to the students, Howard President Wayne A.I. Frederick said he, too, was thinking of a way to honor him. Frederick stated, "Before his death, Chadwick had agreed to serve on the board of the fine arts college and was developing a Master's Class series for students."

On May 26, 2021 Howard University honored Chadwick Boseman's legacy and contribution to keep the college intact by naming the college he fought to preserve after him. Although Chadwick did not live to see those plans through to fruition, his legacy will live on through the newly-named Chadwick A. Boseman College of Fine Arts.

Boseman's family said in a statement, "Chad fought to preserve the College of Fine Arts during his matriculation at Howard and remained dedicated to the fight throughout his career, and he would be overjoyed by this development,"

With the support of Chadwick's wife, Taylor Simone Ledward, and the Chadwick Boseman Foundation, the Walt Disney Company's Executive Chairman Bob Iger, volunteered to lead the fundraising effort to build a state-of-the art facility on the campus and endowment named after Boseman, for Howard University. The new building will house the Chadwick A. Boseman College of Fine Arts, the Cathy Hughes School of Communications, its TV station, WHUT and its radio station, WHUR 96.3 FM.

According to Iger, "Through his tremendous example Chadwick Boseman inspired millions to overcome adversity, dream big and reach beyond the status quo ... and this college named in his honor ... will provide opportunities for future generations of artists to follow in his footsteps and pursue their dreams."

CHAPTER 3

SHARING HIS TALENTS

After graduating from college, Chadwick Boseman moved to the Bedford-Stuyvesant neighborhood of Brooklyn, where he lived at the start of his career, during most of his 20s. He wanted to write and direct, and initially began to study acting in order to learn how to relate to actors. He spent his days in coffee shops — playing chess and writing plays to direct, some of which were influenced by hip-hop and Pan-African theology. Chadwick then attended and graduated from New York City's Digital Film Academy.

Chadwick has had a huge impact on kids from his role as Black Panther, but he was already helping kids years before that. In 2000, he was named a Drama League Directing Fellow. He directed productions including George C. Wolfe's *The Colored Museum* (Wolfe would later direct Boseman in his final role) and a staging of Amiri Baraka's *Dutchman*. After graduating from New York City's Digital Film Academy, Chadwick worked as the drama instructor for the Schomburg Junior Scholars program between 2002 and 2007. This program is housed in the Schomburg Center for Research in Black Culture, located in Harlem, New York. Taking on this role allowed Boseman to pass on his skills and experience as an actor to the young actors of the future, That just shows how much of an inspiring person he was.

Also as a member of the National Shakespeare Company of New York, Chadwick played Romeo in *Romeo and Juliet* and Malcolm in *Macbeth*. He directed and wrote plays as part of the Hip-hop theater movement; his works included *Rhyme Deferred* (co-written with Howard classmate Kamilah Forbes), in which he also performed, and *Hieroglyphic Graffiti*. *Rhyme Deferred* was commissioned for a national tour, as well as featuring in *The Fire This Time* anthology of works, while *Hieroglyphic Graffiti* was produced at a variety of locations, including the National Black Theatre Festival in 2001. Combining modern African-American culture and Egyptian deities, it is set in Washington, D.C. and was picked up by the New York Hip-Hop Theatre Festival and Tennessee State University's summer stock theatre program in 2002. It was also the Kuntu Repertory Theatre's 2002–03 season launch production. At the 2002 Hip-Hop Theatre Festival, Chadwick Boseman also gave a one-man show called "Red Clay and Carved Concrete".

Chadwick rose to prominence as a playwright and stage actor in 2002, performing in multiple productions and winning an AUDELCO award in 2002 for his part in Ron Milner's *Urban Transitions,* which was directed by Woodie King, Jr.

Chadwick with his Parents and actor/producer Woodie King, Jr.

During that same time, Chadwick started to land small parts on New York-based TV shows. He got his first television role in 2003, in an episode of *Third Watch and* in the series *All My Children*. His early work also included episodes of the series *Law & Order*, *CSI:NY*, and *ER*. Chadwick also appeared in episodes of *Cold Case, Lie to Me, The Glades, Castle, Detroit 1-8-7, Justified*, and *Fringe*.

A dramatist as well as an actor, Chadwick continued to write plays. In 2005, Chadwick's stylized, mostly verse play Deep Azure received a full production at the Congo Square Theater in Chicago.

Woodie King, Jr. an American director and producer of stage and screen, as well as the founding director of the New Federal Theatre in New York City was at one of Chadwick's performances and invited the young playright/actor, "Chad", to meet with him at his NYC theatre. So when Chadwick returned home to New York he met with Woodie and got involved with his theatre. Woodie King

Jr.'s New Federal Theatre has given birth to countless playwrights and worked with the best that theater has to offer including Ed Bullins, Amiri Baraka, J.E. Franklin, Ntozake Shange, Ron Milner, and Laurence Holder just to name a few. It has also been the training ground for actors including Chadwick Boseman, Morgan Freeman, Denzel Washington, Debbie Allen, Samuel L. Jackson, Ruby Dee, Leslie Uggams, Jackee Harry, Phylicia Rashad, Glynn Turman, Taurean Blacque, Garrett Morris, Debbie Morgan, Lynn Whitfield, S. Epatha Merkerson, and directors including Lloyd Richards.

Chadwick's play, *Deep Azure* was nominated for a 2006 Joseph Jefferson Award for New Work. *The Joseph Jefferson Award, more commonly known informally as the Jeff Award, is given for theatre arts in the Chicago area. Founded in 1968, the awards are named in tribute to actor Joseph Jefferson, a 19th-century American theater star who, as a child, was a player in Chicago's first theater company. Award recipients are determined by a secret ballot.*

In 2008 Chadwick moved to Los Angeles, the entertainment capital of the world, to solely pursue an acting career. It was a decision that paid off immediately and he never looked back. Shortly after arriving in Los Angeles, Chadwick landed an acting job. He played a recurring role on the television series *Lincoln Heights* and appeared in his first feature film, *The Express,* as Floyd Little. In 2008, he won a Jury Award for Honorable Mention at the Hollywood Black Film Festival. In 2010, Chadwick landed a regular role in another television series, *Persons Unknown*.

The Express (2008)

Chadwick Boseman starred in several successful sports dramas. *The Express* is one is about the real-life story of college football legend Ernie Davis, who was the first African-American to win the Heisman Trophy.

It stars Rob Brown, Dennis Quaid, and Clancy Brown in supporting roles along with Boseman as Floyd Little in one of the actor's earlier movie roles.

After a couple of stagnant years in Los Angeles, Chadwick Boseman returned to New York where he directed an off-Broadway play in East Village. At the time, he was considering giving up acting and pursuing directing full-time. Then, his career took off by leaps and bounds. Chadwick's breakthrough role came in 2013 when he auditioned for the movie *42*, which was a biopic for baseball pioneer, Jackie Robinson, the first African American to play in the major leagues in the 20th century. Robinson played for the Brooklyn Dodgers from 1947 until he retired in 1956. He played in 6 World Series and was a highly acclaimed baseball player. About 25 other actors had been seriously considered for the role, but director Brian Helgeland liked Chadwick's bravery and cast him after he had auditioned twice. In 2013, Chadwick Boseman had also starred in the indie film *The Kill Hole*, which was released in theaters a few weeks before *42*.

The Kill Hole (2013)

In *The Kill Hole*, Chadwick Boseman plays an Iraq war veteran who is forced into finding and killing another veteran.

It's a very tense action movie and it sees Boseman's character really weigh up the moral values of what he is doing, having to follow direct orders even though it means killing a fellow vet. Both men have the same scars from their time in the war, and it makes for a very interesting plot.

42 (2013)

In *42*, Chadwick Boseman is Jackie Robinson, the first African-American to play in Major League Baseball in this highly-acclaimed sports drama. The movie is riveting, tragic, and totally inspiring and it was arguably the performance that made mainstream audiences notice Boseman and his clear talents for the first time.

In 2014, Chadwick's performance in 42 got him named the "Male Star of Tomorrow" by the National Association of Theater Owners.

Suddenly, after ten years in the business, Chadwick was on fire. In addition, prior to their open casting, Universal selected Chadwick Boseman on August 26, 2013 to play the lead role in another high-profile project, *Get On Up*, a movie portraying the personal struggles and successes of music legend James Brown. Chadwick did all of his own dancing and some singing. The soundtrack is a live recording of James Brown's music.

Then, on September 17, 2013 Universal announced an open casting call for actors, musicians, and extras for different roles in the biopic. The auditions were held on September 21st, almost a month after Chadwick had been selected. *Get on Up* was met with positive reviews from critics, with praise mainly going to Chadwick Boseman's performance. The film had a rating of 80% on the review aggregator site *Rotten Tomatoes*, based on 158 reviews, with an average rating of 6.9/10. The site's consensus reads: "With an unforgettable Chadwick Boseman in the starring role, *Get on Up* offers the "Godfather of Soul" a fittingly dynamic homage. *Get On Up* does justice to his unknowable soul and James Brown's unending music, both of which defy closure by definition."

Get On Up (2014)

In *Get On Up*, Chadwick Boseman takes the lead and portrays James Brown in this music biopic. The movie tells the story of the singer's life, from his rise from poverty to being the infamous musician he is known as.

25

Boseman starred alongside Viola Davis, Octavia Spencer, and Dan Aykroyd in an impressively well-acted exploration of the larger than life figure.

Chadwick Bosman was on a roll and he never missed a beat since. That same year, he appeared opposite Kevin Costner in *Draft Day*, in which he played an NFL draft prospect, Vontae Mack. Later in 2014, *Get on Up* was released.

Draft Day (2014)

Draft Day centers around an NFL draft, where General Manager Sonny Weaver tries to rebuild his team. However, he has to decide what's worth sacrificing when he's considering the dreams of hundreds of young men.

Kevin Costner takes the lead in this sports drama but Boseman follows close behind in a strong supporting role alongside Jennifer Garner.

Throughout his career, Boseman was seemingly careful about the stories he wanted to tell and the characters he wanted to play — and though he never let on to the public, he may have known that these roles might be his last.

Message From The King (2016)

In *Message From The King*, Chadwick Boseman takes on the role of Jacob King in this movie, where he travels to Los Angeles looking for revenge and justice against those who were responsible for his sister's disappearance. His character goes from pleasant to incredibly dangerous and it shows just how far people are willing to go when a family is hurt.

Chadwick plays the role really well and the film does a great job at ramping up the tension and the stakes as it goes on.

In 2016, Boseman came back with a vengeance when he starred as Thoth, a deity from Egyptian mythology, in *Gods of Egypt*. Chadwick stated that he had prayed to be the "Black Panther" *before* he was cast as the character in the Marvel Cinematic Universe. Soon after, Chadwick's prayers were answered when he actually started portraying the Marvel Comics character T'Challa / Black Panther, with the blockbuster *Captain America: Civil War* being his first film in a five-picture deal with Marvel.

Gods Of Egypt (2016)

In *Gods of Egypt,* the story sees the God of the underworld take the throne of the ex-king as he looks to take over the land by any means necessary. There's no shortage of action and an obvious good vs. evil plot, but the movie was heavily criticized for having a predominantly white cast playing Egyptian deities.

Captain America: Civil War (2016)

In *Captain America: Civil War* this is the first time we meet Chadwick Boseman as Black Panther. He allies with Captain America, and he definitely helps create one of the most epic superhero battles in movie history.

This movie had fans absolutely stoked for a solo Black Panther movie, which they loved, but they'll always remember this sequel as the battle of the Avengers, as the heroes Iron-Man and Captain America went toe to toe.

The following year, in 2017, Chadwick briefly returned to biographical movies with *Marshall*, where he played Thurgood Marshall (also a Howard University alumni). Thurgood Marshall was an extraordinary Civil Rights attorney who won hundreds of cases, including Brown VS Brown which desegregated all white schools throughout America so that African American students could attend high schools with white children. Thurgood Marshall later was nominated by President Lyndon Johnson Marshall to become the first African American Supreme Court Justice. Marshall sat on the United States Supreme Court from October 1967 until October 1991. He died in 1993.

Marshall (2017)

Marshall began production at the beginning of 2016, the same year that Boseman was diagnosed with stage 3 colon cancer, so he likely learned of his diagnosis while filming or shortly after.

This movie tells the story of the first Black Supreme Court justice, Thurgood Marshall, during one of the most infamous cases in his career, taking place before he becomes the first African-American Supreme Court Justice. The case is about an African-American employee who is accused of attacking his Caucasian boss, and Marshall defends his innocence. Boseman shines brightly in the powerful role.

But it wasn't initially what Boseman thought, given the point in the film where a judge declares that Marshall can't speak in court. Boseman told Roger Ebert of depicting that part of Marshall's story, "It was an extraordinary moment for me because I thought about so many moments where Black people have played in the background and white people who took the credit. And I was like, that's actually an interesting story to expose through Thurgood Marshall. So it became a beautiful film experience."

After *Marshall*, Chadwick continued his role as "Black Panther". He headlined the Academy Award nominated movie, *Black Panther*, which focused on Boseman's character as the King of Wakanda, who was the Black Panther in his home country of Wakanda in Africa. The movie was released in February 2018 to rave reviews, becoming one of the highest-grossing films of the year in the United States. *Black Panther* shattered box office records by raking in an estimated $218 million in the United States alone over the four-day President's Day weekend.

Avengers: Infinity War (2018)

Avengers: Infinity War has the biggest cliffhanger of the entire MCU Black Panther certainly proved his skills in this entry, and it's no question that Chadwick Boseman was perfect for this iconic role.

Black Panther (2018)

Black Panther made serious waves in the world of movies. The superhero will always be the actor's most popular role.

Avengers: Endgame (2019)

Avengers: Endgame was the end of an era in superhero movies in so many ways, bringing a close to the stories of many beloved MCU heroes. Chadwick Boseman returns as Black Panther to close out the huge celebration of the franchise and all its accomplishments,

"A true fighter, Chadwick persevered through it all, and brought many of the films his fans have come to love so much. From *Marshall* to *Da 5 Bloods*, August Wilson's *Ma Rainey's Black Bottom* and several more, all were filmed during and between countless surgeries and chemotherapy."

21 Bridges (2019)

In the gritty crime thriller, *21 Bridges*, Boseman played an NYPD detective who embarks on a citywide manhunt for a pair of criminals who kill numerous cops in a robbery gone wrong.

Starring alongside Sienna Miller and J.K. Simmons, Chadwick carried over plenty of the commanding presence that he exuded in his superhero role as Black Panther.

In 2019 Chadwick was announced as part of the cast for the Netflix films *Da 5 Bloods*, directed by Spike Lee, and *Ma Rainey's Black Bottom*, directed by George C. Wolfe. He took these "bucket-list roles" for opportunities to work with Lee and with *Ma Rainey* producer Denzel Washington, as well as the opportunity to perform in an August Wilson play, telling *Entertainment Weekly* that he wanted to make these non-superhero films because "if you don't do the films that you plan to do, I think you wouldn't feel fulfilled as an artist."

Da 5 Bloods (2020)

Released in 2020, *Da 5 Bloods* ended up becoming one of Chadwick Boseman's greatest movies. This war movie is set during the Vietnam War and follows a group of black soldiers (the Bloods), as they hide gold to retrieve at a later point. The film follows their return journey as they try to find the gold, as well as the remains of one of the fallen members of the group. The film has heart, emotion, action, and a lot of tension, making it truly gripping from start to finish.

Directed by Spike Lee, the July 2020 film was Boseman's last release before his death, and it was hailed by critics. While the movie's subject matter is thought-provoking and timely, Boseman also tried to bring some joy to the set. He posted a video of himself and the cast goofing around on set with Lee. The actor wrote, "Spike was calling a play. But on a hot summer day during water festival, we had an audible. Pure joy."

Chadwick was in Southeast Asia to film his small but pivotal role in *Da 5 Bloods*, what would be his penultimate film. Lee was one of countless people who later, upon finding out Boseman had been battling cancer since 2016, marveled at the actor's physical stamina on set.

"I didn't know Chad was sick," Lee told *Variety* in the fall of 2020. "He did not look well, but my mind never took that he had cancer. It was a very strenuous shoot. I mean, we all didn't get to Vietnam until the end of the movie at Ho Chi Minh City. But that other stuff, the jungle stuff, was shot in Thailand. It was 100 degrees every day. It was also at that time the worst air pollution in the world. I understand why Chadwick didn't tell me because he didn't want me to take it easy. If I had known, I wouldn't have made him do the stuff. And I respect him for that."

In July 2019, Chadwick was off to Pittsburgh to make Ma Rainey's Black Bottom. *In the ensuing year, the couple got engaged and tied the knot. And then, on Aug. 28, 2020, came word that Boseman was gone.*

Ma Rainey's Black Bottom (2020)

Ma Rainey's Black Bottom is the final movie ever released to feature Chadwick Boseman, with this being the last role he filmed before passing away. From 'Marshall' to 'Da 5 Bloods,' August Wilson's

'Ma Rainey's Black Bottom,' and several more, all were filmed during and between countless surgeries and chemotherapy,"

Ma Rainey's Black Bottom, in which Chadwick co-stars as trumpeter Levee, was released after his death in 2020. Director Wolfe said that Chadwick was excited by the role for the challenge it posed, saying that "it's a *monster* role and it's a thrilling role, it's a difficult role. All of those things are exhilarating for an actor. And Chadwick rose to the occasion and more than delivered."

The film is based on the August Wilson play of the same name. Chadwick was a fan of Wilson and wrote about him and his inspiration on Chadwick's own work. The movie is inspired by the career of Ma Rainey, an influential blues singer and the title character as her band gathers at a recording studio in Chicago during the 1920s, which leads to major tension. She argues with her white manager about the control of her own music, while the trumpeter, Levee (played by Chadwick), expresses his desires to start a band, which comes with its own issues. It's a detailed look at the music industry, and the many flaws it had at the time.

Produced by Denzel Washington, Todd Black, and Dany Wolf, the project was originally announced alongside Washington's *Fences* in 2013 as part of his ten-picture deal with HBO. The adaptation eventually moved to Netflix, and filming began in Pittsburgh in 2019.

Ma Rainey's Black Bottom received universal acclaim and Chadwick Boseman received numerous posthumous nominations and awards. Critics lauded the performances of Viola Davis, Chadwick Boseman, and Glynn Turman as well as the costume design and production values. It was named as one of the ten best films of 2020 by the American Film Institute. In all, Ma Rainey's Black Bottom received five nominations at the 93rd Academy Awards, including Best Actor (Boseman) becoming the eighth person (and seventh man) to receive a posthumous Academy Award acting nomination, Best Actress (for Davis), and won two awards: Makeup and Hairstyling and Costume Design. Additionally, the film received eight Critics' Choice Movie Award nominations and nine NAACP Image Award nominations, including Outstanding Motion Picture, with Davis and Boseman both winning lead acting awards. Boseman received British Academy Film Award for Best Actor. Davis and Boseman also won lead acting awards for their performances at the Screen Actors Guild Awards, making history as the first Black actors to win in leading categories in the same year; both received nominations at the Golden Globes, with Boseman posthumously winning Best Actor – Motion Picture Drama.

Sadly, Chadwick Boseman died during post-production in August 2020, making *Black Bottom* his final film appearance; the film is dedicated to his memory. The death of Chadwick Boseman is one that truly rocked Hollywood, mainly because nobody saw it coming. And it was all the sadder as the film was very much intended to center Boseman as an Oscar contender. A superhero both on and off the screen, his passing was truly a heartbreaking moment. Thankfully, Chadwick leaves behind an incredible legacy of movies from his career, having entertained millions in so many different ways.

By so many accounts, Chadwick Boseman led a generous, purposeful and fulfilling life, building his career one carefully considered role at a time, amassing a credit list that included mighty historical figures and a game-changing comic book superhero.

But only after he died, did the lens zoom in on the inner life he'd deliberately kept to himself, his private world suddenly of mass interest. Because learning about what Boseman was like behind the scenes was all that was left to peruse alongside his now frustratingly small body of work that should've had decades more to grow.

CHAPTER 4

BECOMING
THE BLACK PANTHER

Marvel knew Chadwick was meant to play Black Panther, so they didn't even make him audition before casting him for the role. The first of these films was *Captain America: Civil War*. Scarlett Johansson and Chris Hemsworth were among the actors who had to audition for their roles in this film, but the same did not apply for Boseman. Based on his performances in previous films, Boseman was offered the role over the phone by Marvel Universe President, Kevin Feige. Of course, Boseman accepted.

Ironically, Chadwick was one of the few kids who didn't like comic books growing up even though he actually became a superhero in real life years later. Boseman has said that he prayed he would get the role of Black Panther in the Marvel Cinematic Universe months in advance of being cast in the role. Once he landed the role, he read as many comics as he could that related to Black Panther to learn more about the character and his backstory, The comic books obviously must have helped him portray Black Panther since the movie won multiple awards and gained millions of fans.

On top of Chadwick Aaron Boseman being known as the Black Panther, he also has a Xhosa name. Chadwick studied African personalities like Nelson Mandela and Fela Kuti and he traveled to CapeTown, South Africa twice, where the fictional country's accent is based. While he was there, a street musician gave him the Xhosa name 'Mxolisi'. This name means 'Peacemaker', During his time in South Africa, Boseman also learned how to speak a little Xhosa."

Black Panther, released in February 2018, became one of the biggest movies in the Marvel Cinematic Universe (MCU). It now holds the record for biggest February debut and has gone on to have the second-highest second weekend in box office history. Ryan Coogler, the director, dropped a cultural phenomenon in theaters; and moviegoers, who wouldn't normally go see superhero movies, went in droves to see Chadwick Boseman's T'Challa and Wakanda on the big screen.

Chadwick was nominated for his role as Black Panther in *Captain America: Civil War* in 2016 but didn't win any awards until he was the lead role in a Marvel movie in 2018. "Chadwick Boseman was nominated for seven awards, of which he won four. He won two MTV Awards, one for Best Actor in a Movie and the second award for Best Hero. He also won the People's Choice Male Movie Star of

2018 and the Screen Actors Guild Award for Outstanding Performance by a Cast in a Motion Picture,"

Black Panther, was a groundbreaking entry in the Marvel Cinematic Universe with the box office gross and cultural impact to prove it. *Black Panther* was also one of the last movies to be released in Marvel's Phase Three, hitting theaters just before *Avengers: Infinity War*, which set the stage for *Avengers: Endgame* April 2019.

CHAPTER 5

AVENGERS ENDGAME

A *vengers: Endgame* is an American superhero film, based on the Marvel Comics superhero team, the Avengers, produced by Marvel Studios and distributed by Walt Disney Studios Motion

Pictures. It is the sequel to 2012's *The Avengers*, 2015's *Avengers: Age of Ultron*, and 2018's *Avengers: Infinity War;* and it is the twenty-second film in the Marvel Cinematic Universe (MCU).

Avengers: Endgame was announced in October 2014 as *Avengers: Infinity War – Part 2*. The Russo brothers came on board to direct in April 2015, and by May, Markus and McFeely signed on to write the script for the film. In July 2016, Marvel removed the film's title, and it remained untitled until its official title was revealed in December 2018. Filming began in August 2017 at Pinewood Atlanta Studios in Fayette County, Georgia, shooting back-to-back with *Infinity War*, and ended in January 2018. Additional filming took place in the Metro and Downtown Atlanta areas, New York, Scotland and England. With an estimated budget of $356 million, it is one of the most expensive films ever made.

Avengers: Endgame was directed by Anthony and Joe Russo and written by Christopher Markus and Stephen McFeely. The film features an ensemble cast, including: Robert Downey Jr., Chris Evans, Mark Ruffalo, Chris Hemsworth, Scarlett Johansson, Jeremy Renner, Don Cheadle, Paul Rudd, Brie Larson, Karen Gillan, Danai Gurira, Benedict Wong, Jon Favreau, Bradley Cooper, Gwyneth Paltrow, and Josh Brolin, and of course, Chadwick Boseman.

Several actors from *Infinity War* reprised their roles in *Endgame.* In the film, the surviving members of the Avengers and their allies attempt to reverse the damage caused by Thanos in *Infinity War*. In April 2018, Chadwick Boseman, as T'Challa / Black Panther, rejoined his other Marvel cohorts: Captain America, Iron Man, etc. from the movie *Avengers: Infinity War*. *Avengers: Endgame*, was released in April 2019.

Avengers: Endgame was widely anticipated, and Disney backed the film with extensive marketing campaigns. It premiered in Los

Angeles on April 22, 2019, and was theatrically released in the United States on April 26, 2019, in IMAX and 3D. The film received praise for its direction, acting, musical score, action sequences, visual effects, and emotional weight, with critics lauding its culmination of the 22-film story. It grossed nearly $2.8 billion worldwide, surpassing *Infinity War*'s entire theatrical run in just eleven days and breaking numerous box office records, including becoming the highest-grossing film of all time, overtaking 2009's *Avatar*.

CHADWICK'S PHOTO JOURNEY

"LOOKING BACK ON A LIFE WELL-SPENT"

WAKANDA FOREVER

*Marvel Studios made the entire world shout "Wakanda Forever!"
when Black Panther hit theaters in February 2018,
kicking off a spectacular run that made the film one of the highest-
grossing movies of all time, worldwide, with the best reviews of any
movie in Marvel's cinematic universe.*

*Chadwick Boseman graced the covers of Rolling Stone Magazine, gaining high praise for his performance in **The Black Panther**.*

Chadwick portrayed as Marvel's Messiah in Rolling Stone photoshoot

Getting Ready for Action

Michael B. Jordan and Chadwick Boseman facing off in 'Black Panther'

The Unforgettable Four

Chadwick Boseman and Letitia Wright in 'Black Panther'

Black Panther Leading Ladies

Danai Gurira and Florence Kasumba in 'Black Panther'

Chadwick and Lupita congratulating each other at the 25th Annual Screen Actors Guild Awards

(L-R) Sterling K. Brown, winner of Outstanding Performance by a Cast in a Motion Picture for 'Black Panther' and Outstanding Performance by an Ensemble in a Drama Series for 'This Is Us;' Angela Bassett, Lupita Nyong'o, Chadwick Boseman, Danai Gurira, Michael B. Jordan, and Andy Serkis, winners of Outstanding Performance by a Cast in a Motion Picture for 'Black Panther,' pose in the press room during the 25th Annual Screen Actors Guild Awards at The Shrine Auditorium on January 27, 2019 in Los Angeles, California.

Black Panther Cast accepting award for Outstanding Motion Picture at 50th Annual NAACP Image Awards

CHAPTER 6

BLACK PANTHER: WAKANDA FOREVER

Black Panther: Wakanda Forever is an American superhero film based on the Marvel Comics character Black Panther. Produced by Marvel Studios and distributed by Walt Disney Studios Motion Pictures, it is intended to be the sequel to *Black Panther* (2018) and the 30th film in the Marvel Cinematic Universe (MCU). Ideas for the sequel began after the release of *Black Panther* in February 2018.

King T'Challa, had made his debut in *Captain America: Civil War*, starred in his solo film, and then was promptly turned to dust at the end of *Infinity War*. With the box office successes of *Infinity War, Black Panther 1 and Endgame, Black Panther 2* was inevitable. But despite the colossal success of the original *Black Panther* movie, Marvel and Disney never seemed in a rush to bring out the film's sequel…

Obviously, the return of Chadwick Boseman as T'Challa in *Black Panther 2* was thought to be predestined. But, tragically, after the film's leading man died at age 43 in August 2020, following a four-year battle with cancer, the filmmakers had to rethink how a sequel would actually work. Without Chadwick's character, T'Challa, it was clear that the sequel would be very different from the first film.

Black Panther was the first superhero movie nominated for Best Picture at the Oscars. And now, just four years later, fans are wondering *what Black Panther 2* will look like without its iconic King T'Challa. So, it's no surprise that Marvel rehired the first film's writer/director Ryan Coogler to marshal the action.

Marvel head honcho, Kevin Feige, had already expressed his desire to bring back director Ryan Coogler to do *Black Panther 2* before the first movie had even hit theaters. Marvel has made it a habit to stick with certain directors, which made the return of Coogler almost 100 percent. Plus, the director expressed his enthusiasm for working with Marvel a number of times, so we know that the working relationship was there behind-the-scenes. In October 2018, *The Hollywood Reporter* announced that Ryan Coogler would be back to direct the *Black Panther* sequel. According to *THR*'s report, Coogler began working on the script (as of April 2019); and Marvel Studios publicly confirmed Coogler's involvement, August 2019, during Disney's D23 convention.

Ryan Coogler with Marvel Studios President Kevin Feige at Disney's 2019 D23 convention

Officially confirmed to return as the writer and director on *Black Panther 2*, Ryan Coogler indicated that he was well aware of the unique pressure on him to replicate the success of the first *Black Panther* film. "I've had a chance to make three feature films, each one of them had its own very specific type of pressure. In the process of it, it feels insurmountable each time," Coogler told IndieWire. "When it comes to making a sequel, I've never done it before — a sequel to something that I've directed myself. So, I think there's going to be a lot of pressure there, but what we're going to try to do is just focus on the work, like we always do. [We'll] really try to go step by step and try to quiet everything else around us, really focus on trying to make something that has some type of meaning."

Coogler negotiated to return as director in the following months, and Marvel Studios had officially confirmed the sequel's development in mid-2019. Plans for the film changed in August 2020 when *Black Panther* star Chadwick Boseman died, with Marvel choosing not to recast his role of T'Challa. According to Coogler, "I spent the last year preparing, imagining and writing words for Chadwick to say, that we weren't destined to see. It leaves me broken, knowing that I won't be able to watch another close-up of him in the monitor again or walk up to him and ask for another take." However, other main cast members from the first film were confirmed to return by that November, and the title was announced in May 2021. *Black Panther 2* production began in late June 2021, taking place in Atlanta, Georgia, and around Massachusetts.

While the loss of Boseman was devastating, the cast and crew hope to honor him by continuing the story in satisfying ways. Producer Kevin Feige has noted that the plan is to honor the legacy Boseman helped build. "Chadwick Boseman was an immensely talented actor and an inspirational individual who affected all of our lives professionally and personally," Feige said at 2021's Disney investor presentation. "His portrayal of T'Challa the Black Panther is iconic and transcends any iteration of the character in any other medium from Marvel's past. And it's for that reason that we will not recast the character. However, to honor the legacy that Chad helped us build through his portrayal of the King of Wakanda, we want to continue to explore the world and all the rich and varied characters introduced in the first film."

Few details had emerged about *Black Panther 2: Wakanda Forever*, but it was clear that it's going to be very different than the first film. The filmmakers had to rethink how a sequel would work without his character, T'Challa. In December 2020, Disney announced that a new actor would not be hired to fill the role, adding that the new movie would focus on other characters within the world of Wakanda, the fictional African country where T'Challa was king. Disney tweeted, "Honoring Chadwick Boseman's legacy & portrayal of T'Challa, @MarvelStudios will not recast the character, but will explore the world of Wakanda & the rich characters introduced in the first film."

Marvel executive Victoria Alonso has also said the studio has no plans to digitally recreate Boseman's image for the film. "There's only one Chadwick and he's not with us. Our king, unfortunately, has died in real life, not just in fiction, and we are taking time to see how we continue the story and what we do to honor this chapter of what has happened to us that was so unexpected, so painful, so terrible, really."

Ryan Coogler, who signed on to write and direct the sequel after directing and cowriting the first *Black Panther* film, thinks Boseman would want everyone involved in the franchise to press on without him. "I know Chad wouldn't have wanted us to stop," he told *The Hollywood Reporter* in March 2021. "He was somebody who was so about the collective. *Black Panther*, that was his movie. He was hired to play that role before anybody else was even thought of, before I was hired, before any of the actresses were hired."

Lupita Nyong'o, who played Nakia in the first film, agreed with Coogler. "It's gonna be different, of course, without our King to go back into that world, but I know that all of us are dedicated to reimagining or carrying on his legacy in this new *Black Panther* film."

Many original stars are also being featured in the sequel. Returning cast members from the first *Black Panther* include Letitia Wright as Shuri, Danai Gurira as Okoye, Lupita Nyong'o as Nakia, Martin Freeman as Everett K. Ross, Winston Duke as M'Baku, and Angela Bassett as Ramonda. Dominique Thorne will debut as Riri Williams, aka Ironheart, in the movie ahead of the premiere of her own *Ironheart* series on Disney+.

The cast of the original *Black Panther* honored Chadwick Boseman's legacy as they filmed the "Black Panther" sequel. Letitia Wright stated, "We honored him (Chadwick) by committing ourselves to this story that he started, the legacy he started with this franchise. And we just committed every day to working hard, no matter what circumstances we faced. *And we faced a lot of circumstances!* A lot of difficult situations, but we came together as a team and we poured everything into this movie, so I'm excited for you to see it." The 28-year-old actress - who plays the younger sister of the Black Panther, stars alongside Lupita N'Yongo and Martin Freeman.

Production on *Black Panther: Wakanda Forever* was delayed due to the story changes, while COVID-19 also complicated the expected shoot. Even though a final script was not locked in stone, filming began. Production initially took place from late June to early November 2021, in Atlanta and Brunswick, Georgia, as well as around Massachusetts. It wasn't too long after that *Black Panther 2*'s production encountered its first big hurdle, as Wright became unable to continue working after sustaining several injuries during a stunt. While filming continued without her, there was only so much that could be accomplished with the franchise's presumed next star. Wright was then at the center of more controversy due to COVID-19 vaccinations, and *Black Panther 2*'s release date was delayed to late 2022.

Officially named *Black Panther: Wakanda Forever,* the *Black Panther* sequel reached a major milestone and finally wrapped filming. Production resumed at the start of 2022 with Wright healed from her injuries, and the cast and crew recently moved to Puerto Rico for its final stretch. Production resumed by mid-January 2022 and wrapped in late March in Puerto Rico.

The end of filming for *Black Panther: Wakanda Forever* means Marvel Studios has now wrapped one of their most intriguing Phase 4 movies. Since *Black Panther* premiered in February 2018, fans had been clamoring for the sequel. In 2022, they'll finally get their wish. For a long time, the *Black Panther: Wakanda Forever* release date was scheduled for May 2022. Then, following a major Covid-19 induced reshuffle MCU movies confirmed a new *Black Panther: Wakanda Forever* release date: July 8, 2022 but the filming wrapped in June. This was day 117 of a planned 88, showing just how many extra days the cast and crew spent making the film. Doing all of this with strict COVID-19 protocols and still mourning the loss of Boseman certainly made this a challenge for those involved. Despite Chadwick Boseman's untimely death, *Black Panther: Wakanda Forever* will debut in cinemas. The release date was rescheduled for the final time to November 11, 2022. The movie will also be available on Disney Plus at some point – possibly 45 days after its theatrical release, depending on how Disney handles it.

Unfortunately, *Black Panther: Wakanda Forever* is not the sequel anyone would have wanted to make – or see. Even though the movie, now titled Wakanda Forever, is one of the most hotly anticipated on the Marvel Cinematic Universe slates, the tragic death of Chadwick Boseman means that the follow-up will come tinged with sadness.

CHAPTER 7

WINNING BIG

C hadwick Boseman looked like a worthy addition to the MCU, having shined several times during his career in character roles on TV and in films such as *Get on Up*. He had demonstrated a plethora of talents and was more than capable of making a memorable King of Wakanda.

Chadwick Boseman was the first African-American superhero to lead a stand-alone Marvel tentpole in 2018's *Black Panther*. In 2014, he signed a lucrative five-film deal that began with 2016's *Captain America: Civil War* which was to continue through Marvel's Phase 3

During his cameo in *Captain America: Civil War*, Chadwick reportedly earned $700,000. However, when he starred in his own MCU film as the titular character, he was reportedly given $500,000, *plus* a percentage of the film's profits. The Oscar-nominated picture made about $1.3 billion at the box office.

Introducing Chadwick's character in a film that was all but a lock to gross a billion dollars was a smart way to have him gain wide exposure amongst moviegoers, familiarizing audiences with Black Panther and what he's all about. Chadwick Boseman was well-received in the role, which led to more box office profits when *Black Panther* hit theaters.

Chadwick Boseman was locked in for five films with Marvel; a deal that started with a *Captain America 3* role and ran through Phase 3. *Black Panther* was one of the movies he appeared in, leaving three unknowns. Chadwick's tenure in the MCU began not in his own solo film, but in a sequel to an established franchise. Prior to Chadwick's deal, Marvel had introduced their heroes in standalone flicks before crossing them over with other characters, but this marked the first time that a title hero led his/her own movie *after* their cinematic debut.

Since he debuted in Captain America: Civil War, Chadwick Boseman starred in Black Panther and was heavily featured in both

Avengers: Infinity War and Avengers: Endgame, fighting alongside Earth's Mightiest just like the Black Panther character did on the comic pages. This means his extant contract only included one more film, the much-anticipated Black Panther 2.

Black Panther (1) did a great job of teasing footage without giving much away. The first trailer for Black Panther made its debut in June of 2017, which was pretty far in advance of the February 2018 release date. A TV spot was aired first and then there was an official full-length trailer drop at some point afterwards with a few different TV spots as well as an epic Super Bowl commercial in 2018.

Chadwick was nominated for his role as Black Panther in *Captain America: Civil War* in 2016 but didn't win any awards until he was the lead role in a Marvel movie in 2018. He was, however, nominated for seven other awards, of which he won four. He won two MTV Awards, one for Best Actor in a Movie and the second award for Best Hero. He also won the People's Choice Male Movie Star of 2018 and the Screen Actors Guild Award for Outstanding Performance by a Cast in a Motion Picture."

The Marvel blockbuster *Black Panther* was also up for several Academy Awards, including Best Picture, which made it the first superhero movie to achieve that feat. So, it was pretty much a guarantee that you got to see the whole cast of *Black Panther* don their red-carpet best at the awards show on February 24, 2019…and of course they did…in all their splendor!

The movie scored seven total nominations for the 91st Academy Awards. In addition to its milestone Best Picture nod, *Black Panther* was nominated for Original Score, Original Song ("All the Stars"), Costume Design, Production Design, Sound Editing, and Sound Mixing. *Black Panther* became the first Oscar-winning film from Marvel Studios, taking home three awards - for Costume Design, Production Design, and Original Score.

Costume designer Ruth Carter won her first Oscar, cementing her place in Oscar history, as the first African American woman to win in the category. Bringing home the Oscar for Production Design were the duo of Jay Hart and Hannah Beachler, who became the first African-American to be nominated for - and win - in this category. And Ludwig Goransson won his first Oscar for *Black Panther's* original score (which he also won a Grammy for a few days prior!) In his speech, Goransson thanked the film's director Ryan Coogler, with whom he was a student at USC.

Always planning ahead, Chadwick Boseman already had ideas for what to do after *Black Panther.* Originally a screenwriter, Boseman told *Rolling Stone* that he and his writing partner Logan Coles were working on the script for a new movie that *Moonlight*'s Barry Jenkins would direct. "There's a plethora of stories in our culture that haven't been told, because Hollywood didn't believe they were viable," he stated. If *Black Panther* is any indication, though, there's definitely a cultural appetite for more stories about African Americans.

CHAPTER 8

WHAT IF...?

Black *Panther* fans can experience just a little more of Chadwick Boseman portraying the role of T'Challa one last time by watching the new animated series *What If...?* on Disney+.

What If...? is an American animated anthology series created by A. C. Bradley for the streaming service Disney+, based on the Marvel Comics series of the same name. It is the fourth television series in the Marvel Cinematic Universe (MCU) produced by Marvel Studios, and the studio's first animated series. The series explores alternate timelines in the multiverse that show what would happen if major moments from the MCU films occurred differently. Bradley serves as head writer with Bryan Andrews directing.

Each episode features different versions of characters from the MCU films, with many actors reprising their roles for the series. The final two episodes bring together characters from earlier episodes to form the "Guardians of the Multiverse", Among the characters, the show features the voice of Boseman as his iconic character T'Challa in four episodes of the series but is the lead in Episode 2.

The second episode of *What If...?* explores the possibility of what would have happened if T'Challa was taken by Yondu Udonta as a child instead of Peter Quill.

What follows is an action-packed adventure that sees T'Challa become a famous galactic outlaw with the Ravagers, and he travels across the universe to help save worlds from destruction.

T'Challa is so great at saving the universe that he even helps convince Thanos not to collect the Infinity Stones and kill half of Earth's population as happens in *Avengers: Infinity War*. Drawing from *Black Panther* and *Guardians of the Galaxy,* the second episode of *What If...?* proved to be a fitting farewell to Boseman.

What If...? marks the first time Chadwick Boseman voiced the character in an animated project. Sadly, it also marks the last time he got to bring T'Challa to life before his tragic passing.

According to executive producer Brad Winderbaum, "He (Chadwick) was so gracious. We were so fortunate to have him record for the series. He reprises his role as T'Challa in at least four episodes, in different versions of the character reimagined because of the different states of the universe. We had no idea at the time, when he was recording with us, that this would be his final performance as the character. It is such an honor to have had him record, to have his presence in the show. His performance has the same depth and the same impact that it does in live action; he elevates the material in an incredible way. We're so humbled."

Director and executive producer Bryan Andrews said he was eager to work with Boseman on what would, ultimately, be the actor's final performance as T'Challa. "It was amazing," he recalled. "We only got a moment, because our episodes are so short compared to everyone who was able to enjoy his presence on *Black Panther* or even on *Civil War*. We had him for a moment to do our thing, and we're so grateful for it. He was one of the first actors to sign on and say, 'Oh, yeah! I'm going to do that voice.' We were so excited because we really, really wanted to work with Chadwick, and we love *Black Panther*."

Jeffrey Wright, who voices The Watcher, said he met Boseman several years ago at Comic-Con and had hoped to work with him ever since. "It was a lovely surprise to find out that we would have the opportunity to at least be in the same space with *What If...?*," said Wright. "This being his last performance, I find that very moving."

At the end of the episode Marvel paid tribute to the star, writing: "Dedicated to our friend, our inspiration, and our hero Chadwick Boseman."

Chadwick Boseman was diagnosed with stage 3 colon cancer in 2016 and kept his illness a secret. A true fighter, Chadwick persevered through it all and died four years later on August 28, 2020 from the illness at age 43. The episode "What if What If... T'Challa Became a Star-Lord?" aired August 18, 2021. In 2022, Chadwick Boseman received a posthumous nomination at 74th Primetime Emmy Awards, for Primetime Emmy Award for Outstanding Character Voice-Over Performance for the What If...? episode What If... T'Challa Became a Star-Lord?

CHAPTER 9

MORE ABOUT CHADWICK BOSEMAN

Chadwick's Brothers and Parents

Family

Chadwick Boseman was raised Christian and, according to his former pastor, remained a part of the faith. "He did a lot of positive things within the church and within the community," said Pastor Samuel Neely from the Welfare Baptist Church (located at 2106

Bolt Dr, Belton, SC 29627). "With him singing in the choir, with him working with the youth group, he always was doing something, always helping out, always serving. That was his personality."

Chadwick Boseman's family has a longtime history as members of the Welfare Baptist Church, which had its beginnings in 1867, only five years after President Abraham Lincoln signed the Emancipation Proclamation. Like many historically African American congregations, its organization came out of a predominantly white congregation, Neals Creek Baptist Church. The freeing of those who had worshipped under the fig trees of their masters finally became a reality.

On September 5, 1867 thirty-three community leaders, including Catae Rice, Eli Greenlee, Samuel Geer, Ceasar Hammons, Milton Thompson, William Scott, Richmond Ellis, and Carolina Rice united themselves together to form a workable organization. During this meeting, the group invited Reverend F. S. Morris, Reverend H. R. Vandiver, and Reverend J. C. Horton to officiate. After carefully examining the cause for a new congregation with doctrinal principles, Welfare Baptist Church began as an independent Baptist church.

During the following months the first pastor, Reverend Phillip Morris of Anderson, South Carolina, was elected. At the same meeting the first deacons were also elected: Catae Rice, Eli Greenlee, and Milton Thompson.

On October 7, 1871, the church contacted Enoch Vandiver for the purchase of two acres of land, located between Belton and Anderson at a cost of $10.00. The amount of purchase was paid by a loyal member, William Scott.

Reverend Morris exhibited great leadership. Through his dedication and faithfulness of the members, the first building, a log cabin edifice, was built. Reverend Morris resigned in 1970 leaving a congregation exceeding 125 members.

Six pastors served from 1870 until 1890. Each pastor did his very best to teach, preach and lead the congregation to new challenges. In 1890, Reverend J. A. Pinson was elected the seventh pastor of Welfare. Under his tenure, a community leader, James N. Anderson, deeded three acres of land to the church. Like many other African American churches, a schoolhouse was also built. Professor Redman was hired as the principal and teacher.

After setting up an effective program, Professor Redman resigned. The second teacher was Lena Watkins, the daughter of Dr. Harrison Watkins. Upon Mrs. Watkins' decision to leave, Professor Redman returned as principal/teacher. Upon his resignation, Clara McCullough was elected principal to fill the position. Upon completion of her education, Ms. McCullough, now Clara M. Boseman, an early relative of Chadwick's, returned as teacher. Mrs. Boseman was an active member in the Welfare family.

In the early 1930s, a two-room schoolhouse was built. Mrs. Boseman served as principal/teacher and Emma Thompson was hired as a second teacher. These two ladies taught until the school was closed in the 1950s.

In 1901, Doctor Harrison Watkins returned to Welfare as its eleventh pastor. During the late twenties, Doctor Watkin's eyesight began to fail. Soon he became blind. Doctor Watkins died in 1932. Deacons ordained by Doctor Watkins were: Silas Jones, Michael Rice, Henry Dean, Andy Whitner, Henry Ellis, Perry Nance, Henry Peterson, Floyd Brown, Frank Brown, Washington Reid, Franklin

Kay, and M. T. Boseman, who was another early relative of Chadwick's.

In 1934, Reverend Homer Brown of Williamston, South Carolina was elected as pastor. Reverend Brown served for two years. He died in 1936.

In 1936, Revered L. E. Daniel of Belton, South Carolina succeeded Revered Brown. After accepting a position on the staff of Morris College, Reverend Daniel resigned in 1944.

In January 1945, Doctor H. W. D. Stewart of Greenville, South Carolina was elected the fourteenth pastor. Under his administration, the membership built its first brick building. The new building was tri-level, well-lighted, and centrally heated. It was equipped with indoor facilities, a modern kitchen and many Sunday School rooms. The sanctuary was carpeted, and a new piano and organ were purchased. Doctor Stewart resigned in 1962. Deacons serving under Dr. Stewart included: William T. Agnew, W. L. Scott, Joe C. Kay, Cecil Mattison, Ralph Rice, James Boseman, Elliott Boseman, R. M. Boseman, Sylvester Clinkscales, James Dean and Joe Brown.

In 1963, Doctor Moses Patterson Robertson of Pendleton, South Carolina was elected as the fifteenth pastor. Born in Fairfield County, South Carolina, Doctor Robertson successfully pastored several churches before coming to Welfare. Under his leadership the church was renovated with a number of interior and exterior changes. In addition to the renovation, the church witnessed the revitalizing of its program. The following groups were organized: Finance Committee, Trustee Board, Pulpit Aid Auxiliary, Boy Scouts, Young Men's Progressive Club, Men's Chorus, the Inspirational Choir, Young People's Choir, and Children's Choir of which young Chadwick was a member.

On October 2, 1984, Doctor Robertson retired as pastor. Transferred to Welfare were Deacons Donnie Gambrell, Sr. (New Hopewell), and Jone Blanding (Evergreen). Deacons ordained under Doctor Robertson were: W. A. Bolden, A. C. Ellis, Clyde Evans, Mack Nance, William Hunter, Charles Smith and Roger Boseman.

Chadwick's uncle and his father's brother, Mr. Roger Boseman, lived on a street bearing his name, 202 Boseman Road, Anderson SC; he died at the age of 74, on October 26, 2013. He was born in Anderson County to the son of the late Aaron Boseman Sr. and ILove Clinkscales Boseman. He was a member of Welfare Baptist Church. Survivors include his wife Mrs. Ruby Witcher Boseman of the home; two daughters, Regina Boseman Anderson and Claudette Witcher. One son, Stefan Witcher. One sister, Mary McAfee; two brothers, Rev. Tony Boseman and Leroy Boseman. Three Grandchildren. Leroy is Chadwick's father.

On Tuesday, June 25, 1985, at a meeting called by the Board of Deacons, Reverend Samuel Bernard Neely, Sr. was elected the sixteenth pastor. Reverend Neely, a native of Fountain Inn, South Carolina was, at the time of his election living In Mauldin, South Carolina and was pastoring the Mount Zion Baptist Church in Laurens, South Carolina.

Rev. Neely's accomplishments have been many. Under his leadership the remaining mortgage of $86,000.00 was liquidated.. On January 1, 1987, Rev. Neely became the first fulltime pastor of the church. In August of 1987, the existing sanctuary was renovated. The mortgage burning service was held on third Sunday in November 1988. In August 1990, 40 acres of land were purchased at a total of $115,000.00. This addition gave the church a total of 56 acres.

Other than physical improvements, the church grew in its attendance and spiritually. The youth department held its first youth camp during the summer of 1986. The Young Men's Brotherhood was revitalized in 1986. The youth held its first retreat on Hilton Head Island in July 1990. That same year, the youth department, in which Chadwick Boseman had been a member, was reorganized to have its monthly youth services in the old sanctuary. In 1992, Life Support Services, a special anti-drug support program was organized..

The following deacons were ordained under Doctor Neely's administration: Maxie O. Agnew, Sr., J. T. Boseman, a cousin of Chadwick's, Elijah Clemons, Frank Evans, Onice Gray, Jr., Calvin Henry, Sr., Avery James, Jr., Raymond James, Rodney Jones, Willie Lee, Jr., Thomas Ligon, Moffett Martin, Gannie L. McDavid, Sherwin M. Rice, Charles Scott, Undrea Walker, James Ware, and Mahlon Willis. Doctor Neely retired as Pastor of Welfare Baptist Church, February 2015.

In the fall of 2016, Reverend Ankoma Anderson, Sr., of Greenwood, South Carolina, became the seventeenth pastor. His focus has been Welfare, a Church Serving Four Generations. In 2017 Welfare Baptist Church celebrated its 150th Church Anniversary.

Inner Strength

Although Chadwick Boseman had played the leading role in several other biopic movies prior to this year, his dynamic portrayal of T'Challa, the superhero in Marvel's blockbuster 2018 release *Black Panther*, cemented his place in the Hollywood firmament.

But it seems it's no coincidence that Chadwick Boseman, who has portrayed iconic black male figures such as Jackie Robinson (*42*, 2013), James Brown *(Get on Up*, 2014), and Thurgood Marshall

(*Thurgood*, 2017), possesses many of the same qualities of his onscreen characters. He told the *Times* he builds a kind of bridge to these larger-than-life roles through a process of normalizing his subjects to better understand them.

According to the *Times*, "His (Boseman's) method of humanizing superhumans begins with searching their pasts. He's looking for gestational wounds, personal failures, private fears—fissures where the molten ore of experience might harden into steel."

Chadwick with
Mrs. Jackie Robinson

Of course, it also doesn't hurt that the 41-year-old South Carolina native is blessed with chiseled, movie-star good looks and has developed a dogged work ethic and relentless hustle gained through years of scrambling for small roles and writing plays in the New York acting scene. All this paid off once he made the move to L.A.—within two years of switching coasts, he had landed the starring role in *42*.

In November 2019, with *21 Bridges*, a New York City police drama; *Expatriate,* a spy thriller; and the sequel to *Black Panther* on the way, the world finally got to see the full A-list star wattage as well as off-screen intelligence and coolness of Chadwick Boseman.

What made him the man who played men who stood tall? Brian Helgeland, the writer and director of "42," the Jackie Robinson movie that gave Boseman his breakout role, said that the actor

reminded him of sturdy, self-assured icons of 1970s virility, like Gene Hackman and Clint Eastwood.

Chadwick as Jackie Robinson in "42"

"It's the way he carries himself, his stillness — you just have that feeling that you're around a strong person," Helgeland said. He remembered choosing Boseman to anchor his film after seeing only two other auditions. "There's a scene in the movie where Robinson's teammate, Pee Wee Reese, puts his arm around him as a kind of show of solidarity. But Chad flips it on its head. He plays it like, 'I'm doing fine, I'm tough as nails, but go ahead and put your arm around me if it makes you feel better.' I think that's who Chad is as a person."

Lupita Nyong'o, Boseman's co-star and love interest in "Black Panther," described his career choices as those of a socially conscious history buff. She recalled a working session with the film's director, Ryan Coogler, and Boseman that he turned into a mini lecture on the ancient Egyptian iconography and spiritual customs that had informed the original comic book.

"He's very keen to put human experiences in historical context," she said. "Even with a world that was make-believe, he wanted to connect it to the world that we know and could try to understand."

Chadwick said, "They can put the clothes on you," finally, after a long pause. A wry smile fanned across his face — both rows of teeth, steady eye contact. "But then you've gotta wear 'em."

Next up were starring roles in the New York police action drama "21 Bridges" (of which he was also a producer) and the international thriller "Expatriate" (he produced and co-wrote that one).

Remarkably, Chadwick Boseman came this far, despite a relatively late start (he led a studio film for the first time at 35) and while remaining noticeably untouched by the tabloid drama, or whiff of overexposure, that can engulf even seasoned celebrities. In a pop taxonomy of black male nobility, he was cut squarely from the mold of Barack Obama — generally cool, affable, devoted to unglamorous fundamentals — a figure whom he was doubtlessly on a shortlist to portray in an inevitable epic.

For the role of T'Challa, a.k.a. Black Panther, that meant conceiving of a childhood squeezed by the weight of an ancient unbroken dynasty. When it came to becoming Jackie Robinson, he focused on formative years as a Negro League firebrand that crystallized the baseball pioneer's polished exterior. James Brown: a meditation on irrepressible self-confidence, long starved by years of deprivation and insult in Jim Crow South Carolina.

According to Chadwick, "You have to hold it all in your mind, scene by scene. You're a strong black man in a world that conflicts with that strength, that really doesn't want you to be great. So, what makes you the one who's going to stand tall?"

When he was booked for a recurring role in the 2007-9 ABC Family series "Lincoln Heights," which filmed in Los Angeles, it afforded Chadwick his first real taste of Hollywood, which he liked more than he'd expected. Before that, he had just wanted to be an artist in New York, not understanding that going to L.A. and trying to be a film actor was a completely different thing. But he was a quick study. He realized that. *If you've got New York hustle In L.A., what is there to think about?*

As the lead actor in a very prominent mainstream movie with a substantial black cast, Chadwick Boseman had been asked multiple times what his personal feelings were about representation in popular culture.

"Black History Month is extremely important because we actually do need to make people focus on black history at a particular time… because it's not done in our education system," Chadwick said.

"Even sometimes in our churches, it's not done enough. I also feel like we just have a month where we do it. You know? It's my belief that it's something you should do all the time, because black history is part of all of our history."

Politics

Chadwick Boseman put the issue of racism front and center by tackling roles in *42* as Jackie Robinson, the first black baseball player in Major League Baseball, and as Levee in *Ma Rainey's Black Bottom* a musician trying to sell his sound despite his talent falling on the deaf ears of opportunistic white producers.

When it came to taking his views to a big stage like awards shows, Chadwick thought of it as an opportunity, to use his public platform to speak out about injustices not only through the characters that he played, but also in his everyday life. He once stated, "If I can say what I've got to say in 90 seconds, then I should say it. That's why I have the platform. We're here to speak truth to power."

Chadwick was thrust into a media spotlight when cast as Black Panther, a king of a fictional nation in Africa. The very casting gave reporters the opening to ask Boseman about his feelings concerning politics.

However, throughout his career, there was no separating Chadwick's acting work from his politics. In 2017, during the press rounds for *Marshall* he responded to one of the questions, stating, "First of all, I'm not just an actor, I'm an artist. You have to express the full scope of your being, physically, spiritually, and that includes politically, which includes Donald Trump's presidency. In my opinion, if Trump can't take the criticism from the people, don't be the president."

Chadwick supported the "When We All Vote" campaign, and his last tweet before his death was congratulating Kamala Harris on her selection as Joe Biden's vice-presidential nominee. His final social media post highlighted his excitement over Senator Kamala Harris's historic run for vice president. "YES," Boseman tweeted alongside the #WhenWeAll Vote and #Vote2020 hashtags. As an activist himself, it's no wonder Boseman's death also devastated those who echo his calls for social justice. "Heartbroken," Harris posted on Instagram. "My friend and fellow [Howard University] Bison, Chadwick Boseman was brilliant, kind, learned, and humble. He left too early, but his life made a difference. Sending my sincere condolences to his family."

After Chadwick's death, many political figures sent out messages of respect. President Biden tweeted "The true power of [Chadwick Boseman] was bigger than anything we saw on screen. From the Black Panther to Jackie Robinson, he inspired generations and showed them they can be anything they want — even superheroes. There's no doubt that he'll continue to do so, because even though he's no longer with us, the messages and inspiration that he left behind remain. Jill and I are praying for his loved ones at this difficult time."

Advocacy

Outside of performing, Chadwick Boseman supported various charities. After losing his fight against colon cancer, videos and tributes poured in honoring Chadwick Boseman and the inspiration he provided for children battling their own illnesses.

While he was privately battling cancer Chadwick visited children at St. Jude Children's Research Hospital.

After a 2018 visit to St. Jude Children's Research Hospital, Chadwick tweeted, "Had a birthday celebration with a beautiful little princess, Mady. She let me throw the confetti twice. I think I had as much fun as she did."

He worked with cancer charities including St. Jude's Hospital, continuing to support those battling the disease, up until his own death from it. In a message to a producer days before he died, Boseman inquired about sending gifts to childhood cancer patients. St. Jude Children's Hospital tweeted on Sept 12. 2018, "It's not every day that St. Jude gets a visit from an Avenger! Thank you @ChadwickBoseman for stopping by to bring joy to our patients and learn more about our lifesaving mission!"

Chadwick also donated $10,000 to the Boys and Girls Club of Harlem to provide free tickets for children who wanted to see *Black Panther*; he did this to support and promote the Black Panther Challenge started by a New Yorker to raise money for similar children across the country. In response, Disney donated $1 million to the Boys & Girls Clubs to advance its STEM programs. Chadwick advocated for children's charities, with the Jackie Robinson Foundation noting after his death that he helped with their youth outreach. In April 2020, Chadwick donated $4.2 million in personal protective equipment to hospitals fighting the COVID-19 pandemic in black communities, starting his own Operation 42 challenge to encourage others to donate PPE.

In addition to his philanthropic causes, Chadwick advocated for fair and equal pay in the film industry. All of the 21 Bridges' characters were originally conceived as male and white, but Chadwick encouraged amendments to this and other parts of the story. In his capacity as a producer, he sought out Sienna Miller to be his co-star; but she asked for a salary that the studio would not meet. Chadwick then ended up donating some of his salary to get co-star Sienna Miller to the number that she had asked for because he knew it was what she deserved to be paid.

Sienna stated that Chadwick had been really active in trying to get her to do the film. "He was a fan of my work, which was thrilling, because it was reciprocated from me to him, tenfold. This was a pretty big budget film, and I know that everybody understands about the pay disparity in Hollywood, but I asked for a number that the studio wouldn't get to. And because I was hesitant to go back to work and my daughter was starting school and it was an inconvenient time, I said that I would do it if I'm compensated in the right way."

Sienna thought it was unfathomable to imagine any other man in Hollywood behaving that graciously or respectfully.

CHAPTER 10

BEING CHADWICK

Culture writer Steve Rose, in *The Guardian*, said that Boseman's career was revolutionary and he "leaves behind a game changing legacy", attributing this to the actor's careful planning and selection of roles. Eulogizing him, Rose wrote:

Chadwick Boseman began his career playing African American icons and pioneers; he ends it as one himself. His achievements, as an actor and as a cultural force, will surely prove to be as heroic as those of the characters he portrayed. At the very least, he leaves the film-making landscape looking very different to how it was when he entered it.

Looking Regal at the 2018 Met Gala

Presenting at the Golden Globes wearing Versace

Close-up and personal at the Oscar Awards

Hosting Saturday Night Live

Chadwick's Daily Workout Routine

Being an actor is very demanding, mentally as well as physically. The physical part is most obvious because of the variables in the characters you are portraying. Most importantly for Chadwick, playing any superhero was difficult; but when you were playing King of Wakanda, a warrior and the richest superhero, you needed to look your absolute best on screen. Fortunately for Chadwick, even though he was playing the role of a serious superhero, he did not need to be too serious about his diet. Due to his high metabolism, Chadwick always had a lean figure which usually fit with the body type of the characters that he portrayed. Therefore, his diet was not restricted; however, his fitness routine was quite strenuous, but very effective in order to keep him toned and muscle-bound.

Chadwick Boseman worked out 5 days per week:

On day one he practiced gymnastics and core.

- He warmed up with stretches, Pull-ups squats pushups and jogging of 800m.

- Then the intense workout began with circuit 21-15-9.

- Then he performed 21 repetitions of the 2nd ring hold with leg straight.

- Followed by walk plank hold of 21 seconds and inchworms of 21 seconds.

- Next, he performed reverse Superman hold for 21 seconds and 21 planks to push-ups.

- Then he performed 21 lunges. And then in the second round, he performed the above exercises for 15 repetitions or seconds and then in the 3rdround he performed above exercises for 9 repetitions or seconds each.

The second day he performed MMA boxing and cardio.

- His cardiovascular training included long-distance running rowing and cycling.

On the third day, he performed gymnastics and core.

- He started with warming up by stretching pull-ups, air squats push-ups and jogging for 800m.

- Then he started circuit training and repeated all the exercises for 5 times.

- He began with 400m of the run and then followed it by 15 pull-ups and then 25 push-ups.

- Next, he performed 10 handstand push-ups and 5 burpees. (A burpee is done by: Beginning in a standing position; Moving into a squat position with your hands on the ground. (count 1) Kicking your feet back into a plank position, while keeping your arms extended. (count 2) Immediately returning your feet into squat position. (count 3) Standing up from the squat position (count 4).

His fourth and fifth day was an extended part of the above routine.

His Physical Statics.

- He was 6 feet tall and his weight averaged 177 pounds.

- Chadwick's body type was the mesomorph.(Bodies come in different shapes and sizes. If you have a higher percentage of muscle than body fat, you may have what is known as a mesomorph body type. People with mesomorphic bodies may not have much trouble gaining or losing weight. They may bulk up and maintain muscle mass easily).

- His chest was 42 inches, waist was 32 inches and biceps were 16 inches.

- His shoe size was 8.5.

- He had dark brown eyes and black hair.

CHAPTER 11
IT'S A WRAP

Before taking his seat on the Jimmy Kimmel Live! stage, Chadwick Boseman, 40, flashed the *Wakanda Forever* salute from *Black Panther* to the audience.

Wakanda Forever isn't going to forget Chadwick Boseman any more than the rest of the MCU and the fans will. It came as a tremendous shock that a lot of people are still feeling in one way or another when Boseman succumbed to colon cancer not long ago. To say that he was too young to go out in such a way is the type of sentiment that many people have echoed since Boseman's passing. But something else that has been passed along since he was laid to rest is the fact that he effectively hid his condition for so long and managed to keep acting, no matter that the strain on his body must have been excruciating at times. Somehow, Chadwick kept going, and he presented himself as King T'Challa and the Black Panther in a way that inspired more than a few people over the course of his career. Thanks to this, *Wakanda Forever* will be honoring Boseman's legacy. Black Panther will be a part of the movie when speaking of his memory and how it will affect the overall story.

Chadwick had been publicly doing the sign since the immensely popular film released in February 2018. He explained to host Jimmy Kimmel that doing the salute wasn't really an option anymore.

'You know what, the funny thing is, if I don't want to do it, I have to not leave the house. I've been chased in cars, I've actually done the scene in *Coming to America* when he goes to the bathroom and people are bowing to him,' he said.

While Chadwick's enthusiasm for the salute may or may not have been waning, he was surely not tired of those Black Panther checks. Reportedly given $500,000, *plus* a percentage of the film's profits, Chadwick Boseman made about $3 million with the first *Black Panther*. The film itself broke box office records, raking in record amounts. *Black Panther* surprised Marvel Studios and everyone around the world when it became an international phenomenon. Just hours after the hotly anticipated premiere of *Black Panther*, *Vanity*

Fair reported that critics were unified in praise for what was being called Marvel's "first black superhero film." According to *Forbes*, producers spent $200 million to make the movie and another $150 million to publicize it. Their gamble paid off. *Black Panther* lived up to the hype and then some by grossing $400 million domestically in the first 10 days — the second-fastest behind only *Jurassic World*. By the end of February 2018 *Black Panther* had blown past $700 million worldwide to become history's highest-grossing film with a black cast and continued on to make $700,059,566 (domestic) and $646,853,595 (international), totaling $1,346,913,161 (worldwide).

Chadwick Boseman enjoyed success as an actor, playwright, screenwriter and director who became one of hottest names in Hollywood, after starring in the hit movie *Black Panther*. The movie, which had broken a number of box office records over the course of its first two months, was Boseman's most successful role. Prior to *Black Panther,* Boseman reportedly had a net worth of $8 million dollars. This figure came from the actor's previous roles, both on TV and on the big screen.

Chadwick's estimated net worth figure increased following the huge success of *Black Panther*. He reportedly made $700,000 for his first *Black Panther* appearance in *Captain America: Civil War*; add that to what he made from movies like *42* and *Gods of Egypt*. Chadwick Boseman had been a movie and TV star for years, but with the release of *Black Panther* — and the film's critical and box office success — he was in the public eye more than ever.

CHAPTER 12

FINDING THE LOVE OF HIS LIFE

Becoming famous meant a lot of people were talking about whether or not Chadwick had a girlfriend, alongside his magnificent acting talent. While the actor was fairly private on social media, there were clues that suggested the *Black Panther* star might be in a relationship.

The "Black Panther" actor and Ledward were first spotted together at Los Angeles International Airport in 2015. It was speculated that Boseman, who was notoriously private about his personal life, even managing to keep his cancer battle secret, had been dating singer Taylor Simone Ledward.

Of course, the fact that Chadwick and Taylor were seen together didn't prove that they were dating, but a number of tabloids were nevertheless convinced that Chadwick and Taylor were an item. One site suggested that the pair might have been dating for as long as a year, though the two of them hadn't confirmed whether or not they were in a relationship and thus could have simply been friends.

But Both Boseman's and Ledward's families knew about and were supportive of their relationship. "They respect each other. She's very happy, and he is, too," Ledward's grandmother told InTouch Weekly in 2018.

Ledward's sister also gushed about her future brother-in-law. "[Chadwick's] real-life queen is gorgeous, and together they embody true love. Not to mention they would make some beautiful babies," she reportedly wrote on Instagram.

However, on January 27th at the 2019 SAG Awards Chadwick Boseman and Taylor Simone Ledward made a rare awards show appearance together. She was part of the standing ovation when the ensemble went up to accept their win for Outstanding Performance by a Cast in a Motion Picture. Their relationship had become subtly more public as Boseman's rising star gave him more red carpets to walk with his forever-date; so it was likely that they would walk the carpet together again at the Oscars.

Chadwick & Taylor at the 2019 Sag Awards

Chadwick & Taylor at the 2019 Oscars

For quite a while It had been unclear whether Chadwick Boseman was married or not. He had, in the past, been spotted wearing a wedding ring, which went missing from his finger. There were clues that suggested that he might have been in a relationship, but they were not confirmed. He had not been linked to any possible controversy; and managed to keep his personal life, personal, away from the bright and somewhat harmful lights of Hollywood.

The couple was photographed together several times over the years at Hollywood events and often sitting courtside at NBA games.

Most recently, they were spotted during the 69th NBA All Star Game held at United Centre February 16, 2020 in Chicago, IL.

At the NAACP Image Awards in March 2019, the depth of Boseman and Ledward's relationship became well-known to the public. The pair shared a rare moment of public affection when Boseman kissed Ledward before going on stage to accept the award for Outstanding Actor in a Motion Picture.

In his acceptance speech, Chadwick began, "Thank you, God, for not just winning. Thank you, God, for the trials and tribulations that you allow us to go through so that we can appreciate these moments, we can appreciate the joy that comes from winning. 'Cause it's not just me that's winning right now."

He continued, in a nod to the history *Black Panther* had made with its mostly Black cast, Oscar nomination for Best Picture (plus three wins) and billion-dollar box office, "This is a beautiful time in Black filmmaking that we are celebrating right now. It's not just a normal time, we have to recognize that."

Then, he said, "Simone, you're with me every day," reaching out toward her in the audience. "I have to acknowledge you right now. Love you." She blew him a kiss, mouthing back at him, "I love you." *It sounded like they were about to make that love official.*

A few months later, the headlines announced: *He Put A (Big) Ring on It: Chadwick Boseman and Girlfriend Taylor Simone Ledward Are Engaged! Chadwick Boseman is Off the Market.*

Chadwick reportedly proposed to longtime love, Taylor, during the weekend of October 19, 2019, and she said yes. He had popped the question when the couple were on a date in Malibu and they were giddy about taking things to the next level in their relationship.

At the time of engagement, Taylor said that she was very happy and was waiting for this moment for a long time. In early 2020, it was rumored that Denzel Washington told Chadwick Boseman to marry Taylor Simone Ledward during Ma Rainey's Black Bottom Shoot. Denzell recalled to CBS News after Chadwick's death, "I used to watch how she (Taylor) took care of him and I actually said to him, 'Man, you need to put a ring on that finger.' Because she kept her eye on him and she watched him. I'm like, man she loves that guy.

But I didn't know what we know now." Chadwick and Taylor reportedly tied the knot before the film wrapped.

Denzell had observed that Taylor was there not just to support her partner as he shot the 1920s-set drama in the summer of 2019, but also to make sure he was taking care of himself as he threw himself into playing the brash trumpeter Levee, who has high aspirations but is irreparably haunted by family tragedy and the horrors of the Jim Crow South.

Chadwick Boseman wasn't present for his Golden Globe award for his role in *Ma Rainey's Black Bottom* since he finished working on it days before he died. He held on as long as he could so he would be able to inspire people even in the last few days of his life.

Chadwick's family revealed that he had quietly married Taylor in the final months of his life. Chadwick died on August 28, 2020 at the age of 43. The actor's representatives shared the news in a heartfelt tribute on his Twitter and Instagram accounts, revealing he had been diagnosed with stage III colon cancer in 2016 and had battled it as it progressed to stage IV. "It is with immeasurable grief that we confirm the passing of Chadwick Boseman," the Instagram post said. "Chadwick was diagnosed with stage III colon cancer in 2016 and battled with it these last 4 years as it progressed to stage IV."

A statement from Chadwick's family confirmed that the "Black Panther" actor had tied the knot before he died following a four-year battle with colon cancer. "He died in his home, with his wife and family by his side," the statement said. "The family thanks you for your love and prayers and asks that you continue to respect their privacy during this difficult time." Chadwick Boseman died in his Los Angeles home where he lived with his wife Taylor.

Taylor was born on August 31, 1990 in Alameda, California. She graduated from the California State Polytechnic University, Pomona in 2014 with a bachelor's degree in music industry studies. Taylor had also attended Napa Valley College after graduating high school. She began creating music and posting it on social media sites during her college and high school days. She started her musical career as lead singer of her school's jazz band while in college and gave many outstanding performances with the school band while attending the university. Later, she even competed in the world-famous reality show "The X Factor".

Taylor served as the president of the Cal Poly Music Board from 2012 to 2013. She was also the chair of her school's music board; she had begun working as a marketing intern at iHeart Media during this time. Formerly, she had worked at Rockwell as a production assistant at the Los Angeles Philharmonic. She has also conducted orchestra concerts at Walt Disney Concert Hall.

Since Chadwick Boseman's death, Taylor Simone Ledward has been the keeper of his legacy, a role no person mourning the love of her life would ever want but one she gracefully stepped into. Left to speak on his behalf as he was repeatedly honored for what turned out to be his final performance in *Ma Rainey's Black Bottom,* Taylor dutifully cracked open the door so his countless fans and admirers could get a better understanding of the man she knew perhaps better than anybody.

Taylor has been making the rounds bringing everyone to tears and making headlines with her acceptance speeches in his honor. She appeared during the Gothams' tribute to the late actor. At the Gotham Awards, she accepted the Actor Tribute award and gave an emotional speech in honor of her late husband, Chadwick Boseman, in January 2021.

As she came out in public and opened up for the first time since his death, Taylor said, "Keep shining your light on us." She gave an emotional tribute to Chawick while accepting the Actor Tribute honour at the 30th annual IFP Gotham Awards on January 11, saying "As an artist, an actor, and a person, Chad made a practice of telling the truth"; he was the most honest person I'd ever met because he didn't just stop at speaking the truth: he actively searched for it in himself and those around him and in the moment. The truth can be a very easy thing for the self to avoid, but if one does not live in truth then it's impossible to live in line with the divine purpose for your life. And so it became how he lived his life, day in and out. Imperfect but determined," she added.

Taylor continued: "In doing so, he (Chad) was able to give himself over fully in every moment, to be totally present in his own life and in the lives of people he became. He was blessed to live many lives within his concentrated one. He developed his understanding of what it meant to be the none, the one, and the all. He harnessed the power of letting go and letting God's love shine through. Thank you for giving Chad these gifts. It's an honor to receive this award on behalf of my husband, as it was an "acknowledgement not only of his profound work but of his impact on this industry and this world. Chad, thank you. I love you. I am so proud of you."

Additionally, Taylor also accepted the award when Chadwick posthumously won the Golden Globe for Best Actor in a Motion Picture (Drama) for his work in *Ma Rainey's Black Bottom* at the 78th annual ceremony.

Alone on the couch in her golden gown and speaking remotely (like almost everybody else) via Zoom when Boseman won a Golden Globe in February at the pandemic-delayed ceremony, Taylor stated in her speech, "He (Chad) would thank God. He would thank his parents. He would thank his ancestors for their guidance and their sacrifices. He would thank his incredible team...He would thank his team on set for this film...He would say something beautiful, something inspiring, something that would amplify that little voice inside of all of us that tells you, you can, that tells you to keep going, that calls you back to what you're meant to be doing at this moment in history. He would thank [the film's director] Mr. George C. Wolfe, Mr. Denzel Washington, lots of people at Netflix. He would thank Ms. Viola Davis..." She thanked several more before concluding, "And I don't have his words. But we have to take all the moments to celebrate those we love, so thank you, HFPA, for this opportunity to do exactly that. And honey, you keep 'em coming."

Then, accepting on his behalf during the Critics' Choice Awards in March, Taylor admitted, "For those of us who know Chad—intimately, personally, professionally, those he taught, those he gave a word of advice, those who taught him—it is so hard to find a celebratory feeling in these moments, as much as we are proud of him." She concluded invoking a Greek proverb: "'Societies grow great when old men plant trees in whose shade they know they may never sit.' And our society may be a far cry from great, but I know that the seeds you planted will grow into forests."

Not only has Taylor done the impossibly difficult duty of accepting awards on his behalf, but she has also become an advocate for the prevention of colon cancer. In March, Taylor delivered a teary and heartfelt message about the importance of colon cancer screenings as she accepted her husband's award at the 2021 NAACP Image Awards for Outstanding Actor in Motion Picture. The NAACP Image Awards had been the scene of Chadwick's and Taylor's tender moment just two years prior. This time, she used the platform to remind Black people to be vigilant about their health and, if they're at least 45 years old, get screened for colon cancer. A disease that's "beatable," so long as it's caught early enough. "Chadwick was "an uncommon artist and an even more uncommon person," she said. "But the manner in which we lost him is not uncommon at all. Not in our community...Don't put it off any longer, please get screened. Please, you are so needed, and you are so loved. Please take your health into your own hands."

When her husband won Outstanding Performance by a Male Actor in a Film (one of his three nominations) at the SAG Awards in April, Taylor offered, "If you see the world unbalanced, be a crusader that pushes heavily on the seesaw of the mind. That's a quote by Chadwick Boseman."

A few weeks later when the Oscars rolled around, pretty much anybody who'd been paying attention all season was expecting to see Taylor speaking once again from the heart while accepting another well-deserved honor for her husband. But in what will go down as one of the all-time miscalculations in award-show production history, the Oscar for Best Actor—moved so it would be the final award of the night for the first time since the 1940s—went to Anthony Hopkins.

The 83-year-old star of "The Father" was in Wales and reportedly offered to Zoom in to accept, if needed, but—in yet another inexplicable choice—producers turned him down. When he posted his acceptance speech to Instagram the next morning, he made sure to mention Boseman, "who was taken from us far too early." So whatever Taylor may have planned to say if Boseman's name had been called stayed between them instead, no additional statue was necessary to burnish her memories.

And her determination to help prevent more unnecessary loss was evident again when she appeared on the annual Stand Up to Cancer special, which aired Aug. 22, to perform the 1938 standard, "I'll be

seeing you "I'll find you in the morning sun, and when the night is new," Taylor sang, "I'll be looking at the moon, but I'll be seeing you." They weren't her words or his, but they fit just the same.

The relationship between Chadwick Boseman and his wife Taylor Simone Ledward was private. Like their relationship, Taylor, who has handled her loss with grace and dignity, is also pretty private.

However, Simone lovingly shared her late husband's words used to describe himself as, 'A vessel to be poured into and out of.' She stated, "He realized that when one is able to recognize that when their strength does not come from themself, they rarely mess up. That's what he was doing when he was acting. (He) was not merely telling a story or reading lines on a page but modeling a path to true fulfillment."

Although Chadwick knew for several years he had terminal cancer, he died without writing a will, but he made a key move months before his death to financially protect his wife. Taylor got nearly $1 million in personal property and assets, but that's not a true reflection of his wealth and success. The majority of his assets were being held in separate private trusts. Chadwick Boseman's wife, Taylor Simone Ledward, was appointed the executor of the estate in court after his death; but she still had to fight in court to be paid back for expenses related to her husband's funeral. In April 2020, Taylor filed an inventory and appraisal of Chadwick's estate which revealed that it was listed as being worth $3,577,861.

The judge made his final decision on Taylor's request in a hearing set for November 2020; but finalizing a settlement took much longer. In June 2022, nearly two years after "Black Panther" actor Chadwick Boseman died of colon cancer at the age of 43, his family settled up plans to distribute his multimillion-dollar estate. Boseman's widow, Taylor Simone Ledward, requested that the court evenly distribute her late husband's estate equally between her and her in-laws, Leroy and Carolyn Boseman — 50% to her and the other half to his parents. And since Boseman reportedly did not have a will when he died Aug. 28, 2020, his estate was responsible for paying higher legal fees than if he had. The documents revealed that the estate was valued at $3.8 million before court fees, taxes, funeral costs and additional lawyer payments were subtracted. After all the bills are handled, the balance of his estate was $2.3 million.

Boseman is survived by his wife, parents and brothers Kevin and Derrick. According to current accounts, Boseman's widow — the musician Taylor Simone Ledward — asked the court to split his $2.3 million estate evenly between herself and his parents. There have not been any reports so far of inheritance-related conflict between Boseman's widow and his parents, or among any of his surviving relatives.

REMEMBERING "CHAD"

Chadwick Boseman died at his Los Angeles home as a result of complications related to colon cancer on August 28, 2020, with his wife and family by his side.

A public memorial service was held on September 4, 2020, in Anderson, South Carolina, where the speakers included Boseman's childhood pastor as well as Deanna Brown-Thomas, daughter of James Brown, whom Boseman portrayed in *Get on Up*. Chadwick Boseman was put to rest at Forest Lawn Memorial Park in Anderson, SC. The city announced plans for the creation of a permanent art memorial at the service.

Chadwick Boseman became an international superstar after playing T'Challa in 2018's Black Panther, and he allowed so many young people to finally see themselves in a Marvel superhero movie. Not only did he film the strenuous movie while disabled, but Boseman also continued to show up to press events and interact with fans, despite the physical demands of his cancer diagnosis.

While Chadwick Boseman starred in all sorts of movies and portrayed many different kinds of characters, most people likely know him from his Marvel character, Black Panther. As Boseman said in an interview with Esquire, playing Black Panther involved a ton of training and physical work, so it's mind-boggling that Boseman managed to keep up while battling cancer. He stated, "I mean, it's refreshing. It's a relief. I enjoy doing what I do with Black Panther, but I also enjoy not having to put on a suit or train like a professional athlete," he said. "You know, this is the type of movie that I enjoy watching the actors that I love do. It's kind of like, you want to see how you would do it. And not in a copying way, but in a, 'How do I define this in my own way?' So it was great to have that challenge, and to have something that was unfamiliar to me that I can dive into."

Wakanda Forever isn't going to forget Chadwick Boseman any more than the rest of the MCU and the fans will. On August 29, 2020, the day after Boseman died, the tweet in which his family announced his death on his Twitter account became the most-liked tweet in history, with over six million likes in under 24 hours, and accumulating over seven million by August 31.

It came as a tremendous shock that a lot of people are still feeling in one way or another when Boseman succumbed to colon cancer not long ago. To say that he was too young to go out in such a way is the type of sentiment that many people have echoed it since Boseman's passing. But something else that has been passed along since he was laid to rest is the fact that he effectively hid his condition for so long and managed to keep acting, no matter that the strain on his body must have been excruciating at times. Somehow, Chadwick kept going, and he presented himself as King T'Challa and the Black Panther in a way that inspired more than a few people over the course of his career. Thanks to this, *Wakanda Forever* will be honoring Boseman's legacy. Black Panther will be a part of the movie when speaking of his memory and how it will affect the overall story.

Marvel Studios president and CCO Kevin Feige said, "Chadwick Boseman was an immensely talented actor and an inspirational individual who affected all of our lives professionally and personally. His portrayal of T'Challa the Black Panther is iconic and transcends any iteration of the character in any other medium from Marvel's past. And it's for that reason that we will not recast the character. However, to honor the legacy that Chad helped us build through his portrayal of the king of Wakanda, we want to continue to explore the world and all the rich and varied characters introduced in the first film."

Letitia Wright walked the purple carpet for the "Black Panther: Wakanda Forever" premiere, paying tribute to the late Chadwick Boseman by wearing a crystal-embellished suit that brought back memories of Boseman's 2018 Oscars outfit.

A hero both on-screen and behind-the-scenes, Chadwick Boseman will forever be remembered as King T'Challa in Marvel's Black Panther. Upon hearing news of their castmate's unexpected death, Boseman's fellow Avengers took to Twitter to honor his legacy. "Chadwick was special," Captain America's Chris Evans tweeted. "A true original. He was a deeply committed and constantly curious artist. He had so much amazing work still left to create. I'm endlessly grateful for our friendship."

"All I have to say is the tragedies amassing this year have only been made more profound by the loss of [Chadwick Boseman]," Mark Ruffalo, who plays the Marvel Cinematic Universe's Bruce Banner, tweeted. "What a man, and what an immense talent," he added. "Brother, you were one of the all-time greats and your greatness was only beginning. Lord love ya. Rest in power, King."

Brie Larson, who plays Captain Marvel, also tweeted: "Chadwick was someone who radiated power and peace. Who stood for so much more than himself. Who took the time to really see how you were doing and gave words of encouragement when you felt unsure," she wrote. "I'm honored to have the memories I have. The conversations, the laughter. My heart is with you and your family." As Larson added, it's clear that Boseman "will be missed and never forgotten" among those with whom he worked so closely in recent years.

Chadwick's *Ma Rainey* co-star Viola Davis stated, "he (Chad) is going to be remembered as a hero", both as the Black Panther and for the authentic man he was, and "his legacy, his body of work, his integrity, is going to influence on generations upon generations to come."

Many other celebrities and fellow entertainers paid tribute to the accomplished actor on social media following the announcement of his death, including a number of his Marvel Cinematic Universe co-stars.

Kevin Feige called Boseman's death "absolutely devastating", writing: "Each time he stepped on set, he radiated charisma and joy, and each time he appeared on screen, he created something truly indelible. Now he takes his place [as] an icon for the ages."

Viola Davis also mourned him in a tweet, writing, "Chadwick... no words to express my devastation of losing you. Your talent, your spirit, your heart, your authenticity... It was an honor working beside you, getting to know you. Rest well, prince."

"A warrior of light til the very end," Scandal alum Kerry Washington penned. "A true king. I am without words. May he rise in power."

Ryan Reynolds said, "What a brutal loss."

Comedian Wanda Sykes wrote, "I am broken. Praying for his family."

Avengers star Chris Pratt stated on Instagram, "This is such devastating news. We're praying for his family. The world has lost an immeasurable talent and a great person."

This Is Us star Sterling K. Brown said, "I don't have words. Rest In Peace, Bruh. Thank you for all you did while you were here. Thank you for being a friend. You are loved. You will be missed."

Others honored Boseman's legacy in the film industry as well as his activism, like singer-songwriter John Legend, who tweeted, "He brought grace, elegance and power to everything he did. He always seemed to carry our ancestors with him. And now he joins them far too soon."

Real Housewives of Potomac star, Monique Samuels, shared photos of her son's Black Panther-inspired birthday party, writing, "Like wow I'm in tears and they won't stop. Just thinking about what his role did for black kids across the globe."

Writer Clint Smith tweeted, "I keep thinking about my 3-year-old in his Black Panther costume. How he wore it almost every day when he got it, refused to take it off. The way he walked around saying 'I'm the Black Panther.' How happy it made him. What Chadwick gave us was immeasurable. What an enormous loss."

Podcast host Patrick Monahan also wrote, "Thinking about all the stuff Chadwick Boseman made and did after a devastating diagnosis and in the midst of what must have been absolutely grueling treatments. And all that with no one outside his circle catching on at all. Truly an amazing talent. What a cruel, cruel loss."

Activist Bernice King, daughter of Martin Luther King, Jr., also celebrated the impact Boseman's legacy will have on the Black community for generations to come. "We never know what people are enduring. Humans...we are wonders," she tweeted. Thank you, Chadwick, for gifting us with your greatness in the midst of a painful struggle." Her brother, Martin Luther King III, added that, despite his four-year battle with colon cancer, Boseman "kept fighting and he kept inspiring. He will be missed."

His alma mater, Howard University, tweeted in reaction that "his incredible talent will forever be immortalized through his characters and through his own personal journey from student to superhero".

Rhea Combs, film curator of the Smithsonian National Museum of African American History and Culture, said that with his screen presence, Boseman "was not only a conduit to the past and the way African-Americans persevered and pushed through so many challenges, he also represented brightness and the promise of tomorrow".

Major League Baseball and the Los Angeles Dodgers, the franchise for which Robinson played when the team was at its former home of Brooklyn, New York, issued statements honoring Boseman, in light of his acclaimed portrayal of the player. Several publications noted Boseman died on the observance of Jackie Robinson Day, seven years after his having portrayed Robinson.

According to film critic Owen Gleiberman of *Variety*, "Boseman was a virtuoso actor who had the rare ability to create a character from the outside in and the inside out [and he] knew how to fuse with a role, etching it in three dimensions. That's what made him an artist, and a movie star, too. Yet in *Black Panther*, he also became that rare thing, a culture hero".

Peter Bradshaw wrote of the actor's "beauty, his grace, his style, his presence. These made up Chadwick Boseman's persona [and he became] the lost prince of American cinema, glorious and inspirational".

As the Black Panther, Boseman led a predominantly black cast in a major blockbuster for the first time; *Variety* said that "the significance of Chadwick Boseman to the African American and Black community is immeasurable."

Further expressing the weight of Boseman's legacy, Robert Daniels wrote for *Vulture* that "his performance [as T'Challa] wouldn't just be a demonstration of craft, It'd become a piece of history. He'd face a slew of pressures, because a Black epic, even a period piece, is forever expected to be *important*, representative of the past, present, and future." He told BBC Culture that "through his acting, [Boseman] wrote, rewrote, and reclaimed black history".

BBC Culture called Chadwick Boseman "a film icon who changed Hollywood"; "a symbol of black excellence and of cinematic excellence"; and "a virtuoso and heroic figure, not just because of his iconic turn as Marvel's Black Panther but for how he raised the bar for racial equality and representation on screen." The BBC also noted his impact of infusing African authenticity into his work, including his motivations for taking a role in *Gods of Egypt* as well as how T'Challa is presented, saying that he "connect[s] African-American audiences with their African heritage".

On August 28, 2020, a Change.org petition was started, seeking to replace a Confederate monument in his hometown of Anderson with a statue of Boseman; it collected more than 50,000 signatures in less than a week, surpassing its original goal of 15,000 signatures. Henry McMaster, the Governor of South Carolina, ordered the Statehouse flags be lowered to half-staff on August 30 in honor of Boseman, who was born and raised in the state. ABC (which, like Marvel Entertainment, is owned by Disney) aired a commercial-free version of *Black Panther*, followed by a special about Boseman's life and work titled *Chadwick Boseman — A Tribute for a King* on the same day. Also aired on August 30 was the 2020 MTV Video Music Awards; the ceremony was dedicated to Boseman. On September 24, 2020, Disney unveiled a mural titled *King Chad*, by artist Nikkolas Smith dedicated to Boseman at Downtown Disney in Anaheim, California. In February 2021, another mural dedicated to Boseman was painted at Trilith Studios in Fayetteville, Georgia, by artist Brandon Sadler. Following his Best Actor win over Boseman at the Academy Awards in April 2021, Anthony Hopkins said, "I want to pay tribute to Chadwick Boseman, who was taken from us far too early, and again thank you all very much."

Boseman is memorialized in the 2020 video game *Marvel's Spider-Man: Miles Morales*. The game includes an after-credits message dedicating it in memory of Boseman, Along with a touching tribute in the end credits of *Spider-Man: Miles Morales*, Chadwick Boseman also gets a street named after him in the *Spider-Man: Miles Morales* game's version of New York City. Boseman Way is located on a stretch of the game's 42nd Street, between 3rd Avenue and 1st Avenue. The number 42 bears significance in the *Miles Morales* universe as well as referring to Boseman's portrayal of Jackie Robinson. A Wakandan flag also appears. Amazon also made *Black Panther* comic titles available for free on its ComiXology platform in the wake of Boseman's death. On November 29, 2020, Marvel changed the studio's logo animation in the opening of *Black Panther* on Disney+ to include images of Boseman from the film, as well as his appearances in *Captain America: Civil War*, *Avengers: Infinity War*, and *Avengers: Endgame*, to honor what would have been Boseman's 44th birthday.

Chadwick's death has been a tremendous loss for the film industry and the many people around the world who cherished and admired him and, of course, the people closest to him—his adoring family. His oldest brother Derrick Boseman who is a pastor in Murfreesboro

Tennessee added that his baby brother was incredibly talented saying, "He's probably the most gifted person I've ever met. In addition to his talents as a storyteller and an actor his faith was at the core of who he was." This faith was also a great source of comfort to Chadwick during the final stages of his illness. Pastor Boseman recalled the haunting words his sibling uttered the day before his untimely passing, "Man, I'm in the fourth quarter, and I need you to get me out of the game." At that time, the Pastor remembers that he shifted his prayers from "God heal him, God save him" to "God, let your will be done," which allowed Chadwick to pass peacefully the following day.

Chadwick's brother, Kevin Boseman explained to NYT that anything Chad put his mind to he could accomplish. "He always did his best, and his best was incredible."

On October 14, 2020, shortly after less than two months after his younger brother's death, Kevin Boseman, announced, "Today marks my official two-year remission anniversary. I was diagnosed with cancer in 2018 and underwent four rounds of chemotherapy. I'm in remission!!!!!" Similar to Chadwick, Kevin said he initially did not share the news publicly but felt this time of remission is something "to smile about" and something "to shout about" in a year full of so much tragedy. (Chad) I hope you're smiling and shouting with me."

Cancer is something most of us have no control over. We can only control our responses to it, which includes being proactive about our healthcare, both physically and mentally. Tomorrow is not promised, and early detection saves lives. Health is wealth. True wealth.

ABOUT THE AUTHORS

TONY ROSE

Tony Rose, an NAACP Image Award Winner for Outstanding Literature, is the publisher of Amber Books and Colossus Books, the nation's #1 African American Book Publisher of self-help books and entertainment biographies. Tony Rose's Colossus Books imprint has published numerous biographies about internationally-acclaimed Grammy-award winning artists, including **Prince; Jay-Z; Beyonce; Tupac Shakur; Rick James: Dr. Dre; Eminem; Black Eyed Peas; Lady GaGa; Nicki Minaj; New Kids**

on the Block; Notorious B.I.G. and **Suge Knight.** The Amber Books imprint has published numerous historical and self-help books, including ***Tracing Our Roots*** and ***Obama Talks Back – Global Lessons, A Dialogue with Today's Young Leaders..*** Other notable books written and published by Tony Rose include: ***How to Be in the Entertainment Business; African American History in the United States of America; An Autobiography of an American Ghetto Boy;*** and ***America – The Black Point of View.*** (www.amberbookspublishing.com)

YVONNE ROSE

Yvonne Rose is a highly-requested book publishing consultant and an advisor to countless self-published authors who aspire to turn their manuscripts into professionally published books. As the director of Quality Press, the #1 African American book packaging company, Yvonne gives each client a personal consultation, answering all their questions regarding the rules and regulations and the ins and outs of the book publishing industry.

In addition, Yvonne is an award-winning author and has **ghost-written and co-written** several top-selling non-fiction titles, including: *Rising up from the Blood: A Legacy Reclaimed—A Bridge Forward The Autobiography of Sarah Washington O'Neal Rush, The Great-Granddaughter of Booker T. Washington* (Solid

Rock Books) by Sarah Washington O'Neal Rush; *Natural Radiance: A Guide for Ethnic Skin Care* (Global Skin Solutions Publishing) by Pamela Springer; *Fighting for Your Life: The African American Criminal Justice Survival Guide* (Amber Books) by John Elmore, Esq; *Let Them Play...The Story of the MGAA* (MGAA Books) by John David; *A Journey that Matters: Your Personal Living Legacy* (Lyceum Group Books) by Erline Belton; *The Messman: A World War II Hero Tells His Story of Survival and Segregation on the Battleship North Carolina* (Quality Books) by Yvonne Rose and John Seagraves; *FREEZE: Just Think* about It (More Than A Pro Books) by former Phoenix Cardinal, Levar Fisher; and *Seven Ways to Make the Grade* (Bob Lee Enterprises) by Doctor Bob Lee, WBLS Radio, New York City, Television host and Personality. (www.qualitypress.info)

CPSIA information can be obtained
at www.ICGtesting.com
Printed in the USA
LVHW071246221122
733773LV00008B/191